SUMMER ACTIVITIES for Fall Readiness

KINDERGARTEN

Jeanine Manfro

Printed in USA

GARLIC PRESS

Educational Materials for Teachers and Parents

899 South College Mall Road
Bloomington, IN 47401

www.garlicpress.com

Publisher: Douglas M. Rife
Author: Jeanine Manfro
Art Director: Michelle Ste. Marie
Illustrator: Marilynn Barr
Interior Design: Jocelyn Foye
Cover Design: Joanne Caroselli

ISBN 978-1-9308-2050-0
GP-201
TPS, Newton, IL 05 13

Table of Contents

Introduction

Summer is a time when families can relax and enjoy lots of great adventures together. It is also a time when many children forget much of what they learned in the previous school year. This workbook was developed to help children maintain the academic skills they have already acquired and to get a head start on the skills they will learn in the coming school year.

COMMON CORE STATE STANDARDS

Summer Activities for Fall Readiness supports the Common Core State Standards Initiative (CCSS). These standards were developed by teachers, administrators, and educational experts nationwide to ensure that all students are provided with a top-quality education. The standards have been adopted by nearly every state and they provide clear and consistent information about what students should learn at each grade level.

SHORING UP SKILLS AND SETTING SAIL

Help your child sail into Kindergarten with confidence! With just 10 to 15 minutes a day, this workbook can be completed over the summer and your child will enter the school year ready to learn.

The book is divided into 10 one-week sections. Five reading/language arts pages and five math pages are provided for each week. The first half of the book is dedicated to reviewing preschool skills and the second half provides a sneak-peek at what your child will learn in Kindergarten. Pages are clearly marked so that you'll know at a glance if your child is working on a **preschool skill** or a **Kindergarten skill**.

At the bottom of each page, there is a suggestion for an additional activity that you and your child can complete together to extend the learning even further.

Here are just some of the **Common Core State Standards** addressed in this workbook:

Reading/Language Arts

- Letter and Word Recognition
- Phonics
- Rhyming Words
- Sight Words
- Nouns, Verbs, and Adjectives
- Identifying Key Ideas and Details in Stories
- Understanding Informational Texts

Math

- Comparing Sizes
- Shapes
- Patterns
- Identifying Numbers and Counting
- Classifying Objects
- Addition
- Subtraction
- Time and Calendar

A Sea of Stories

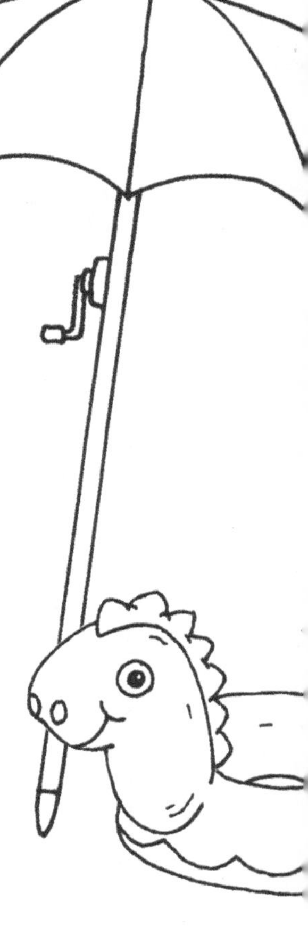

Reading aloud to your child is perhaps the best way to prepare for Kindergarten. Here are some wonderful books to get you started!

FABULOUS FICTION

Blackout by John Rocco. Hyperion, 2011.

Boy + Bot by Ame Dyckman. Knopf Books for Young Readers, 2012.

Chicka Chicka Boom Boom by Bill Martin, Jr. and John Archambault. Simon and Schuster, 1989.

Don't Let the Pigeon Drive the Bus by Mo Willems. Hyperion, 2003.

Down on the Farm by Merrily Kutner. Holiday House, 2005.

A Home for Bird by Philip C. Stead. Roaring Brook Press, 2012.

How to Babysit a Grandpa by Jean Reagan. Knopf Books for Young Readers, 2012.

Kindergarten Rocks! By Katie Davis. Harcourt, 2005.

Miss Bindergarten Gets Ready for Kindergarten by Joseph Slate. Puffin, 2001.

Mouse Paint by Ellen Stoll Walsh. Harcourt, 1989.

Rumble in the Jungle by Giles Andreae. Tiger Tales, 2001.

SuperHero ABC by Bob McLeod. HarperCollins, 2008.

KNOCK-OUT NONFICTION

Actual Size by Steve Jenkins. Houghton Mifflin, 2004.

At This Very Moment by Jim Arnosky. Dutton, 2011.

A Cool Drink of Water by Barbara Kerley. National Geographic Children's Books, 2006.

Clothesline Clues to the Jobs People Do by Kathryn Heling. Charlesbridge, 2012.

Fish Eyes: A Book You Can Count On by Lois Ehlert. Sandpiper, 1992.

It's Harvest Time! by Jean McElroy. Little Simon, 2010.

My Map Book by Sara Fanelli. Harper Festival, 1995.

Somewhere in the World Right Now by Stacey Schuett. Dragonfly Books, 1997.

Swirl by Swirl: Spirals in Nature by Joyce Sidman. Houghton Mifflin, 2011.

This Is the Way We Go to School by Edith Baer. Scholastic, 1992.

Time for a Bath by Steve Jenkins. Houghton Mifflin Harcourt, 2011.

The Watcher: Jane Goodall's Life with the Chimps by Jeanette Winter. Schwartz & Wade, 2011.

A Boatful of Books

MONTH

SUNDAY	MONDAY	TUESDAY	WEDNESDAY	THURSDAY	FRIDAY	SATURDAY

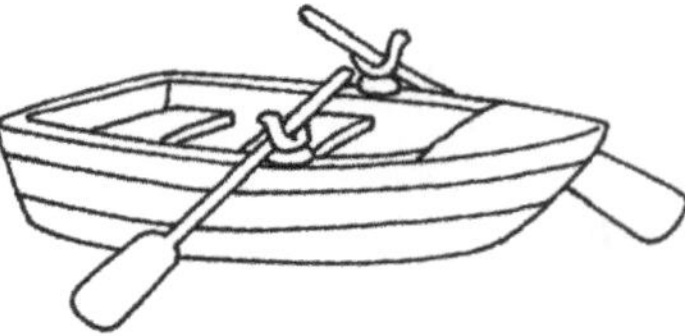

Make three copies of this page—one for June, one for July, and one for August. List the books that you read to your child during each month. Make it your goal to read together every day. Plan a special reward for the end of the summer when you reach your goal.

Fall Readiness Checklist

Children entering Kindergarten should be able to do these things. Check the box for each skill your child has mastered.

READING SKILLS

- ☐ Understands that text is read left-to-right and top-to-bottom.
- ☐ Knows how to hold a book and turn the pages, one at a time.
- ☐ Sings the alphabet song.
- ☐ Knows letters of own name.
- ☐ Names some other letters.
- ☐ Names words that have the same beginning sound (*sun, sand, summer*).
- ☐ Identifies and names rhyming words.
- ☐ Distinguishes between individual sounds in words (dog: /*d*/ /*o*/ /*g*/).
- ☐ Uses new words in conversations.
- ☐ Answers questions about stories.

MATH SKILLS

- ☐ Sings number and counting songs and rhymes.
- ☐ Identifies numbers 1 to 10.
- ☐ Counts objects to 10.
- ☐ Identifies simple shapes.
- ☐ Sorts objects by certain attributes (size, color, shape, etc.).
- ☐ Sequences objects by size.
- ☐ Determines more or less of a quantity.
- ☐ Recognizes and repeats patterns.
- ☐ Matches similar objects.
- ☐ Understands the concepts of yesterday, today, and tomorrow.

Kindergarten Words

Here is a list of words that Kindergartners may learn to read and write. These are based on the Dolch list of frequently used words. Please remember that your child does not need to know these words prior to beginning Kindergarten. They are provided here only as a reference.

a	do	it	red	want
all	down	jump	ride	was
am	eat	like	run	we
and	find	me	said	well
are	for	must	saw	went
at	four	my	say	what
ate	funny	new	see	where
away	get	no	she	white
be	go	not	so	who
big	good	now	soon	will
black	have	on	that	with
blue	he	one	the	yellow
brown	help	our	there	yes
but	here	out	they	you
came	I	play	this	
can	in	please	three	
come	into	pretty	to	
did	is	ran	too	

Baa, Baa, Black Sheep

Listen to the nursery rhyme.

Baa, baa, black sheep, have you any wool?
Yes, sir, yes, sir, three bags full:
One for my master, one for my dame,
And one for the little boy who lives down the lane.
Baa, baa, black sheep, have you any wool?
Yes, sir, yes, sir, three bags full.

- Traditional

Talk about it.

1. Who has three bags of wool?
2. What do you think the wool will be used for?
3. What is a master and a dame? See if you can find out!
4. Circle the words in the rhyme that start with b.

Trace and write.

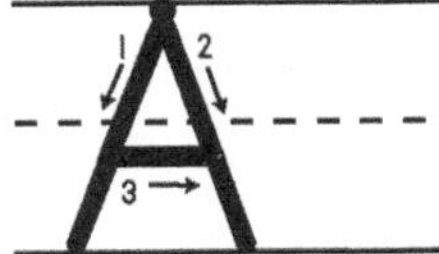

If your child has ever pet a live sheep before, ask how the wool feels. Explain that wool is used to make things such as socks, sweaters, and blankets. If possible visit a farm or petting zoo.

Big and Small

Look at the pairs of pictures. Which one is big? Which one is small? Color the big pictures blue. Color the small pictures red.

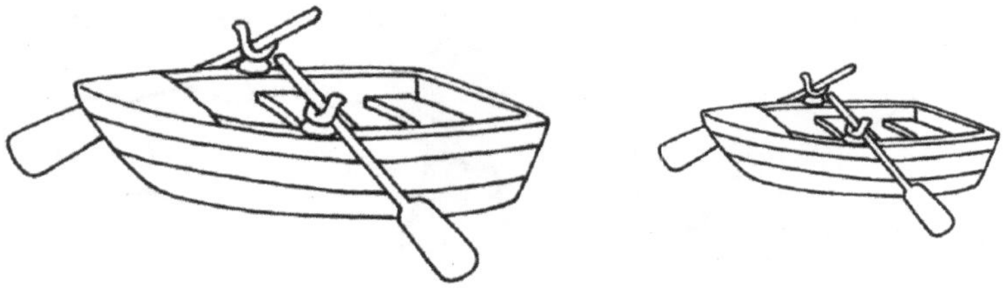

1.

2.

3.

4.

5.

Help your child compare the sizes of different items found at home (examples: big and small shoes, big and small toys). Have your child measure the items with fun things like noodles, cereal pieces, or blocks. Encourage your child to make comparisons such as, "This shoe is smaller. It is three blocks long, and this one is seven blocks long."

Ladybug Letters

Color the ladybugs with letters red.
Color the ladybugs with words blue.

B be T
F am and
M on P
R S
can go Z

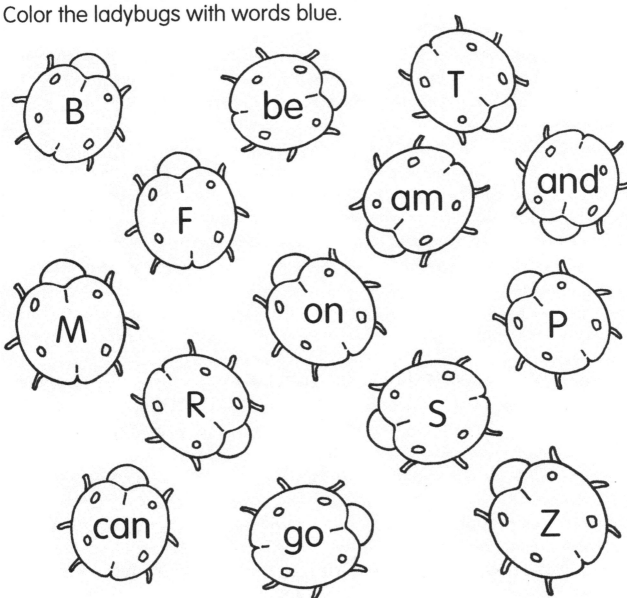

Trace and write.

B B

Have your child find things around the house that begin with the same letter as his or her first name.

Tall and Short

Circle the tallest animal in each row.

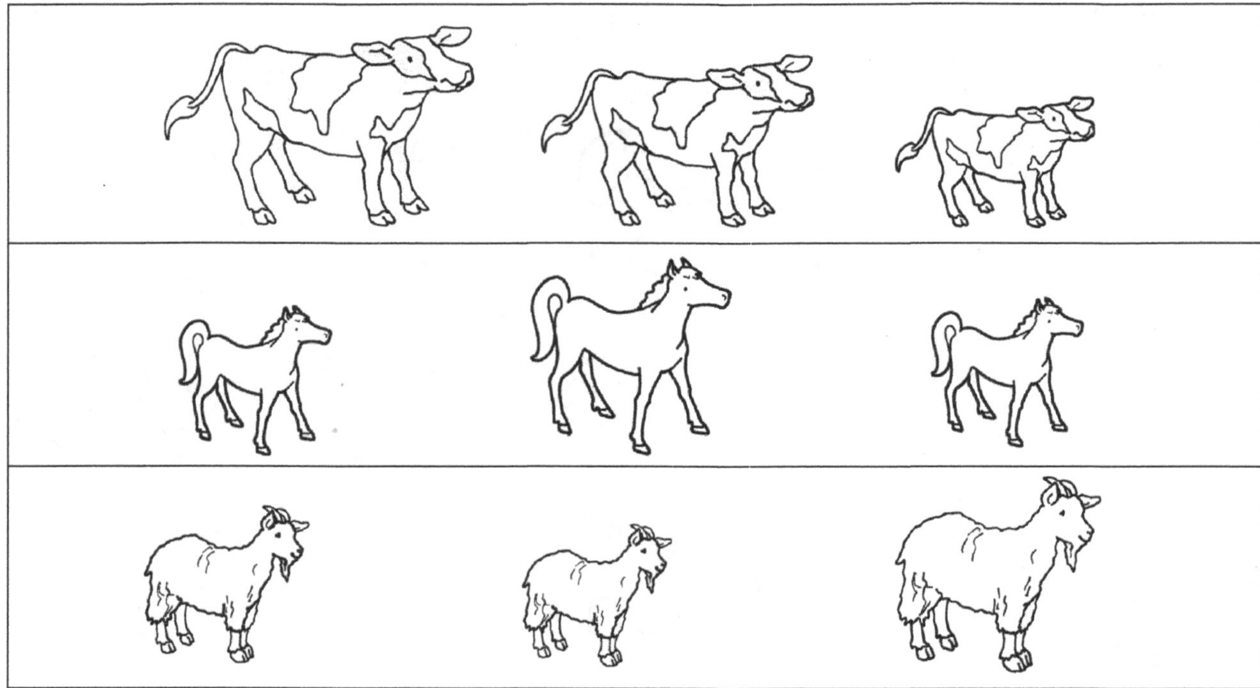

Put an X on the shortest animal in each row.

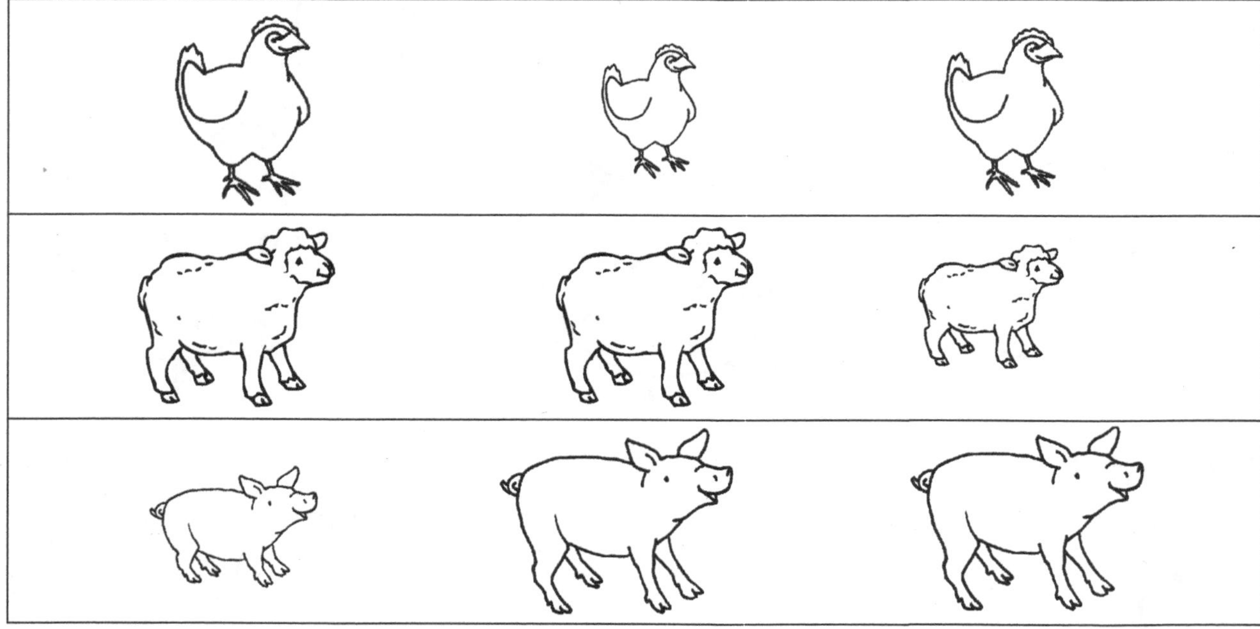

Use family photographs to reinforce the concept of *short* and *tall*. Encourage your child to make comparisons such as, "Grandpa is taller than Aunt Lisa. Grandma is shorter than Mom."

Who Lives in the Woods?

Listen to the poem.

Who lives in the  ? (trees)

Squirrels do.

Who lives on the  ? (rocks)

Lizards do.

Who lives in the 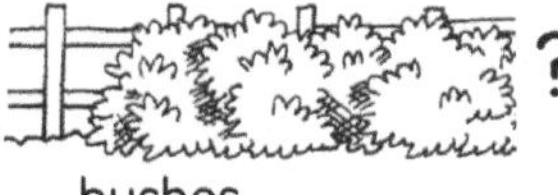 ? (bushes)

Deer do.

Who lives in the  ? (pond)

Frogs do.

Who lives in the  ? (log)

Skunks do.

Who lives in the  ? (burrow)

Rabbits do.

Who likes to visit the woods? **We do!**

Talk about it.

1. Where do all of these animals live?
2. Which animal lives in the pond? What other animals do you think live there too?
3. Tell about a time when you have seen one of these animals.

Trace and write.

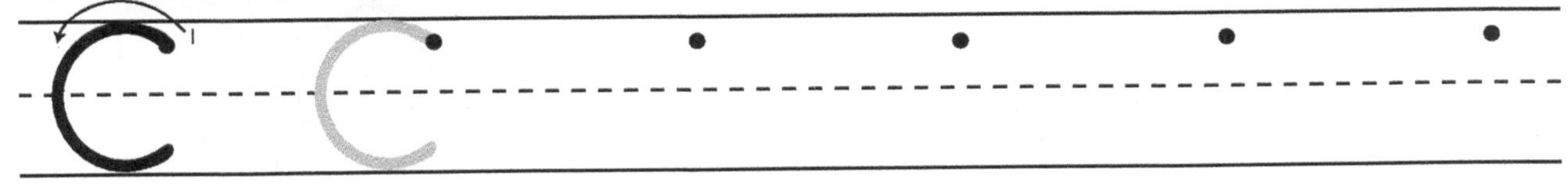

Help your child find photographs of each animal listed here. Talk about how each animal's physical characteristics help it to live successfully in the woods.

Long and Short

Look at the pictures. Draw a line from the short picture on the left to the matching long picture on the right.

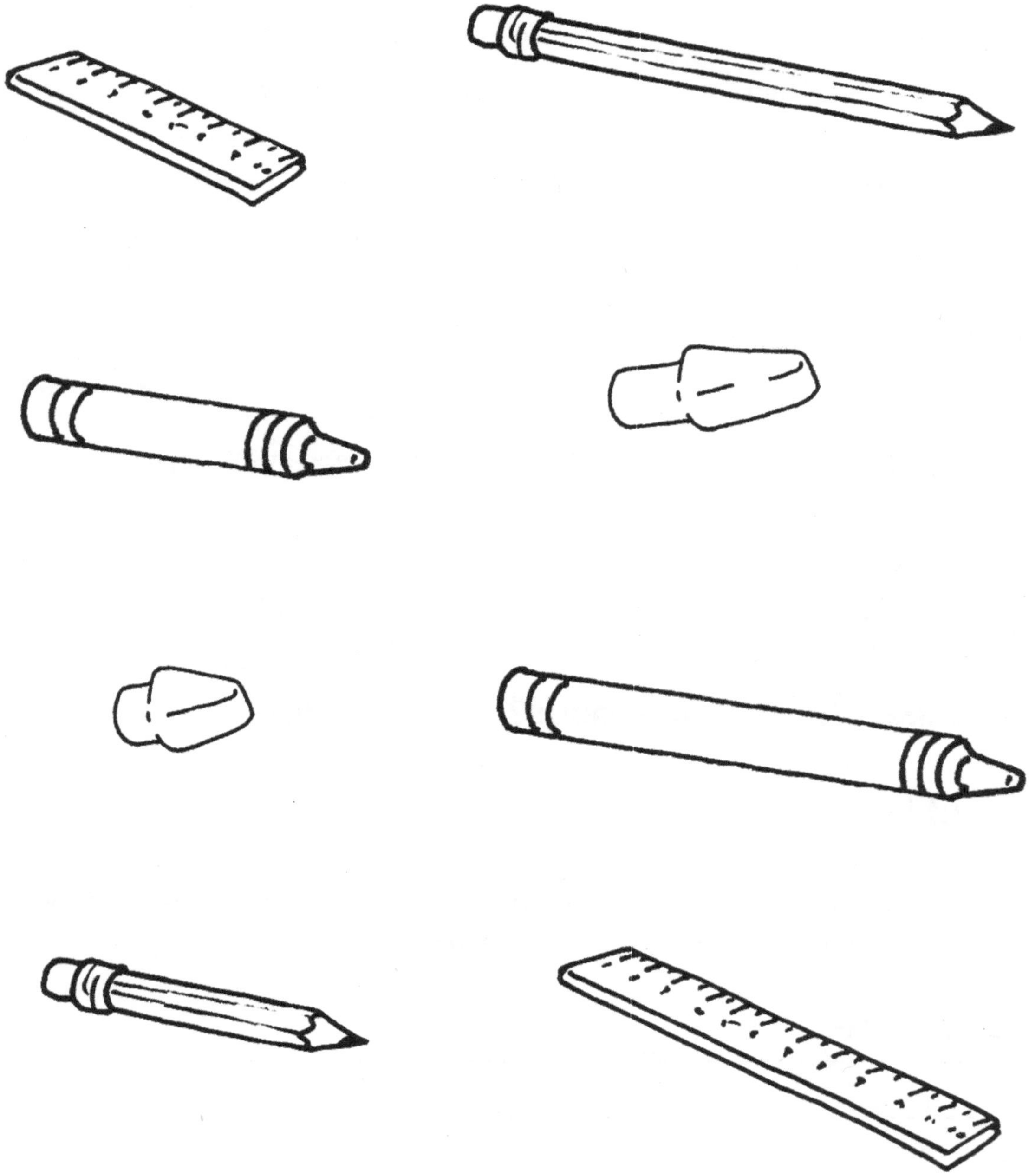

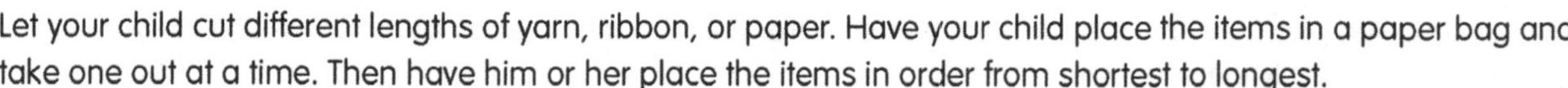

Let your child cut different lengths of yarn, ribbon, or paper. Have your child place the items in a paper bag and take one out at a time. Then have him or her place the items in order from shortest to longest.

She Sells Seashells

Color the shell if you can name its letter. Circle the shell if you can not name the letter.

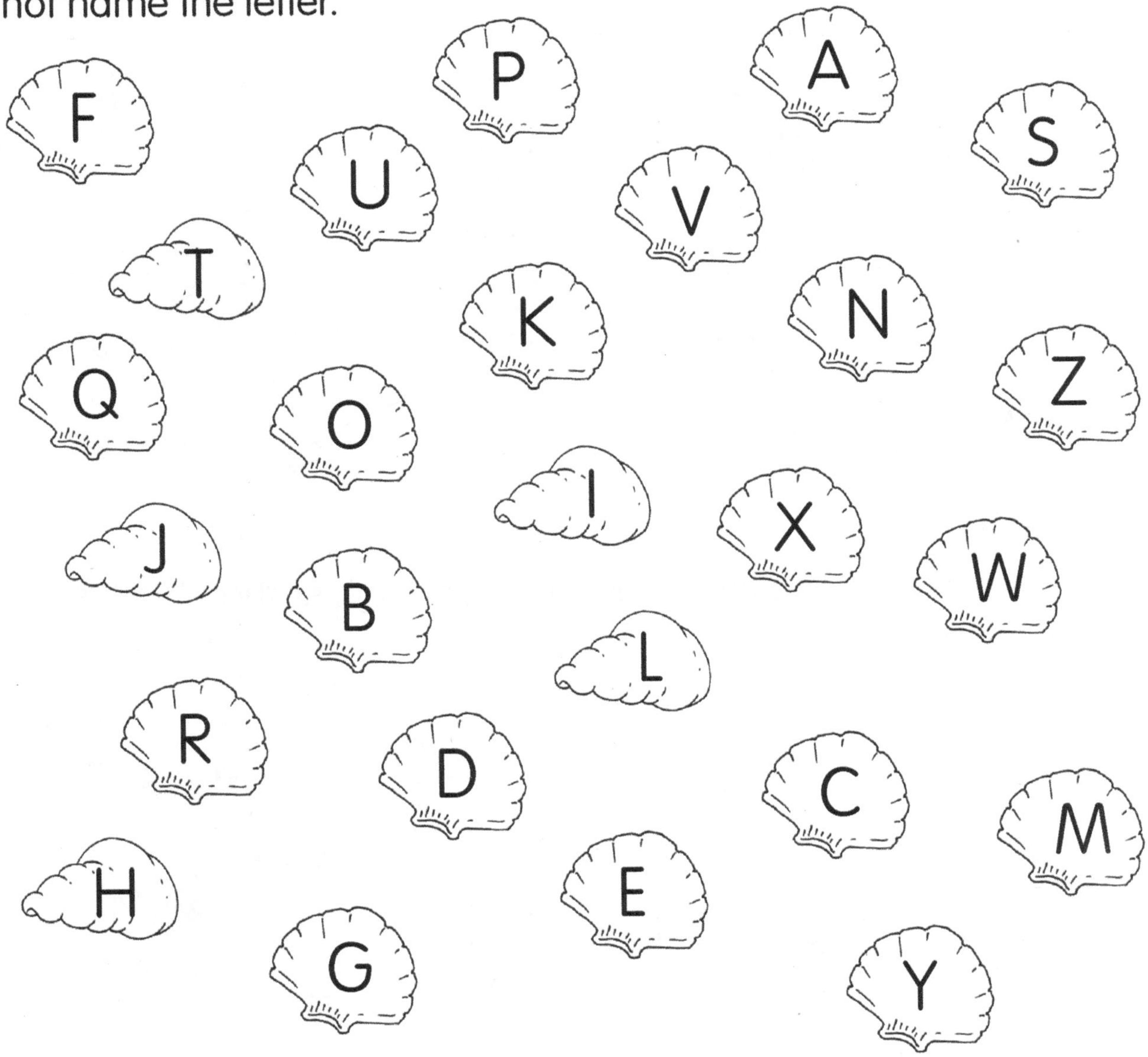

P A F S U V T K N Q Z O I X J W B L R D C M H E G Y

Trace and write.

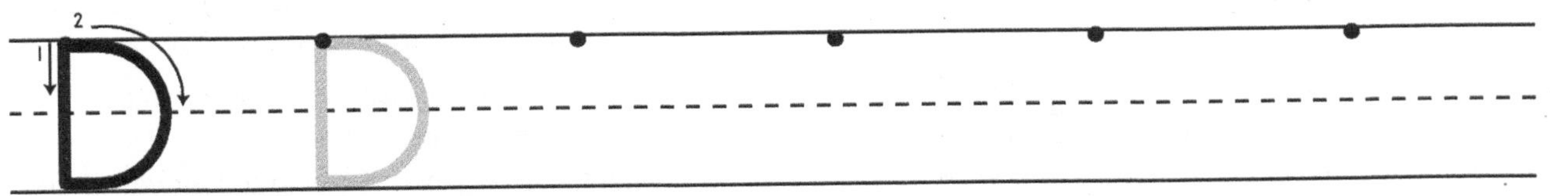

Cut letter shapes out of sand paper. Have your child place a sheet of paper over each letter and rub a crayon over the top. Help him or her place the letter rubbings in ABC order.

Heavy and Light

Look at the pictures. Color the picture that is heavier than the first picture in each row.

Look at the pictures. Color the picture that is lighter than the first picture in each row.

Follow these instructions to help your child make a simple balance scale: 1. Use a plastic coat hanger that has hooks at each end. Tie an empty strawberry basket to each hook. 2. Roll a small amount of modeling dough into a ball. Tie the ball to the center of the hanger so that it acts as a weight. 3. Hang the hanger in a doorway or on a shower curtain rod. 4. Have your child choose different items to weigh. Have him or her predict which will be heaviest and place the items in opposite baskets. The heavier item will cause the basket on the balance scale to tilt down.

The ABC's

Listen to the poem.

A, B, C, D, E, F, G

Do you know the ABC's?

H, I, J, K, L, M, N, O, P

Can you read along with me?

Q, R, S, T, U, V

Almost there. Now end with glee!

W, X, Y, and Z

You just said the ABC's.

Talk about it.

1. What is this poem about?
2. Circle the letters that you can name.
3. Read the poem aloud with someone else. Point to the letters and words as you read.

Trace and write.

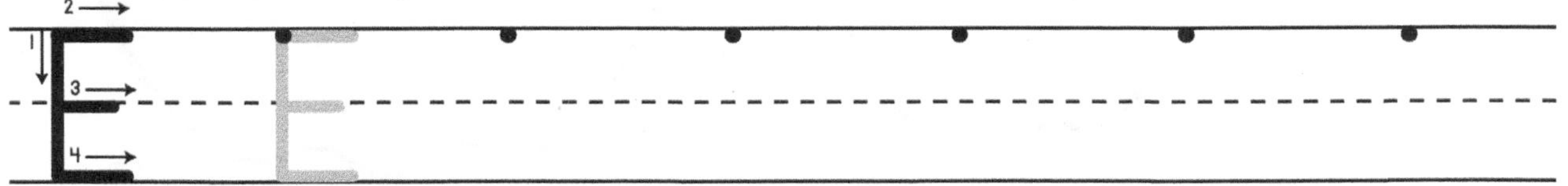

Give your child a set of magnetic letters. As you slowly read the poem aloud, have your child find each letter and stick it on the refrigerator or a metal baking sheet. Then have him or her practice pointing to the letters and saying their names in order.

An Apple A Day

Find the apples that are the same size. Use a different color to color each pair of matching apples.

Collect various pieces of clothing from around your house and place them in a laundry basket. Have your child sort the clothes by size and put same-sized items together. Talk about which members of your family wear the shortest socks, the biggest shirts, the longest pants, and so on.

Humpty Dumpty

Listen to the nursery rhyme.

Humpty Dumpty sat on a wall,
Humpty Dumpty had a great fall;
All the king's horses,
And all the king's men,
Couldn't put Humpty together again.

- Traditional

Talk about it.

1. Where was Humpty Dumpty at the beginning of the rhyme?
2. Why do you think he fell?
3. What do you think happened next?
4. Circle all the words in the rhyme that have at least one **a** in them.

Trace and write.

Cut an egg shape from construction paper. Let your child decorate the egg to look like Humpty Dumpty before his great fall.

Circle Time

Trace the circles. Color them yellow.

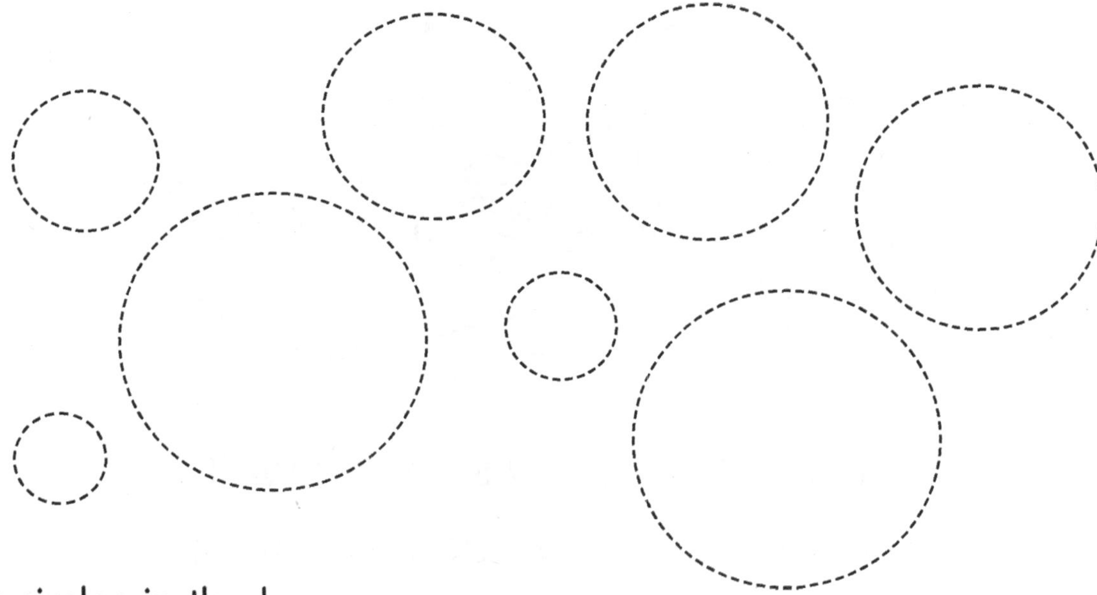

Draw circles in the box.

Have a "polka-dot party!" Let your child use a variety of materials to make circles of different sizes. Try things like dot markers and paper, cookie cutters and modeling dough, cotton swabs and ink pads, and scissors and wrapping paper.

A Good Egg

Draw lines to match the uppercase and lowercase letters.

j h q D E
d e L l m Q
A g F R J
a B H c n
N M C G b f r

Trace and write.

b b

Make a memory match game using uppercase and lowercase letters. Choose six letters to begin. Write each uppercase letter and its matching lowercase letter on separate index cards. Shuffle the cards and arrange them face down in even rows. Take turns turning two cards over at a time to find matching pairs.

Super Squares

Trace the squares. Color them green.

Draw squares in the box.

Cut squares from sheets of construction paper. Have your child sort the squares by size and color. Then have him or her glue them to a sheet of paper to make a collage.

How to Brush Your Teeth

Listen to these steps on how to brush your teeth. You should brush every day after breakfast and before bedtime.

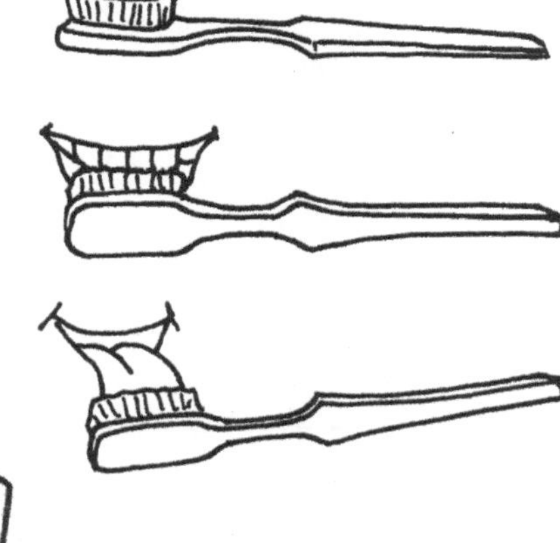

First, put a small dab of toothpaste on your toothbrush.

Next, brush every side of every tooth.

Don't forget to brush your tongue!

Then, rinse with water.

Finally, use dental floss to clean in between your teeth.

Talk about it.

1. When should you brush your teeth?
2. What is the first step in brushing your teeth?
3. Should you brush only the fronts of your teeth?
4. Why do you think you need to brush your tongue?

Trace and write.

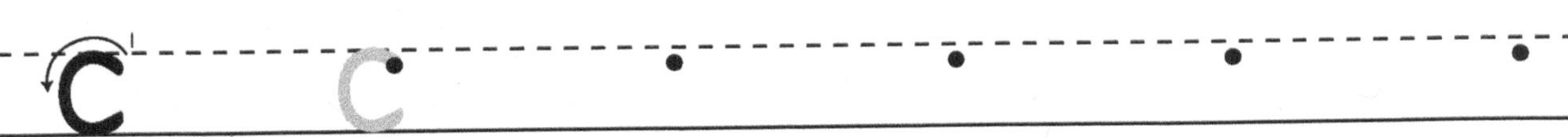

Copy this page and put it in the bathroom. Print a tooth-brushing chart from the Internet. Let your child mark the chart every time he or she follows the steps shown here.

Terrific Triangles

Trace the triangles. Color them orange.

Draw triangles in the box.

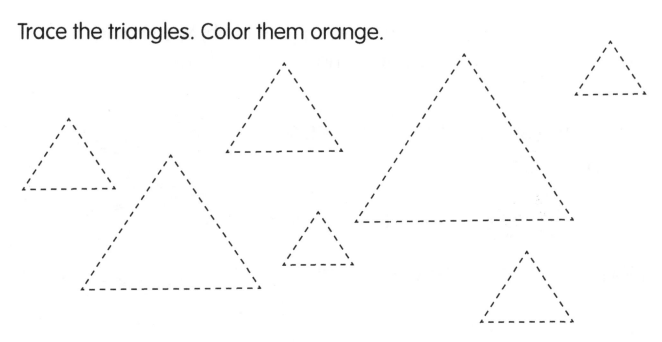

Using a child-safe knife, encourage your child to cut various soft foods into triangle shapes. Try slices of bread, sandwich cheese, tortillas, pancakes, and cooked lasagna noodles.

Don't Fall

Connect the dots.

Trace and write.

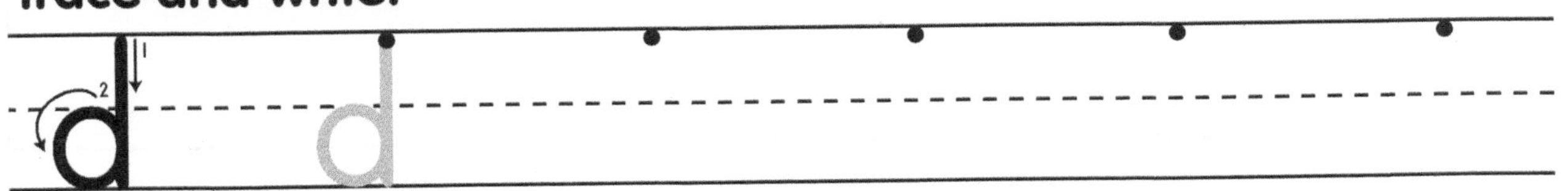

Use chalk to write a lowercase **a** on the sidewalk. Ask your child to write the letter that comes next in the alphabet. Take turns writing the letters until the whole alphabet has been written.

Remarkable Rectangles

Trace the rectangles. Color them purple.

Draw rectangles in the box.

Collect empty food boxes. Have your child feel and describe the shape of each box. Then have your child glue the boxes together to make a sculpture.

On the Farm

Listen to the poem.

Pigs by the barn.  Horses by tree.

Goats by the fence.  Cows by me.

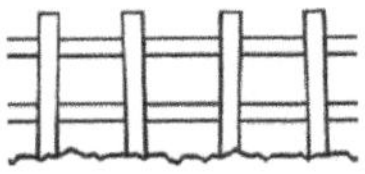

Sheep by the house.  Dogs by the chair.

Chickens by the garden.

Animals everywhere!

Talk about it.

1. Where do the animals live?
2. Which of the animals can probably go inside the house?
3. Color the pictures.
4. Circle the words. Touch and read each word.

Trace and write.

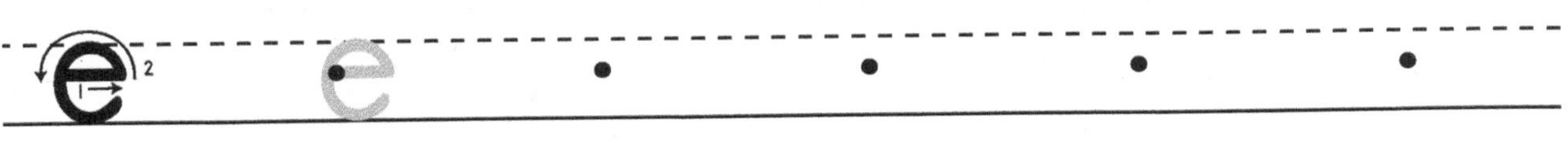

Write the sight words **by** and **the** separately on ten different index cards. Have your child collect different objects from around the house and arrange them with the phrase **by the** to create simple sentences to read. For example, *spoons by the forks, books by the shoes,* and *papers by the pens.*

Ship Shape

Use the code to color the picture.

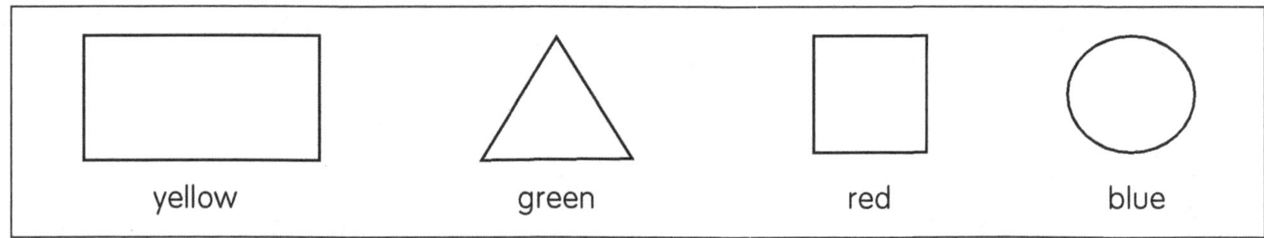

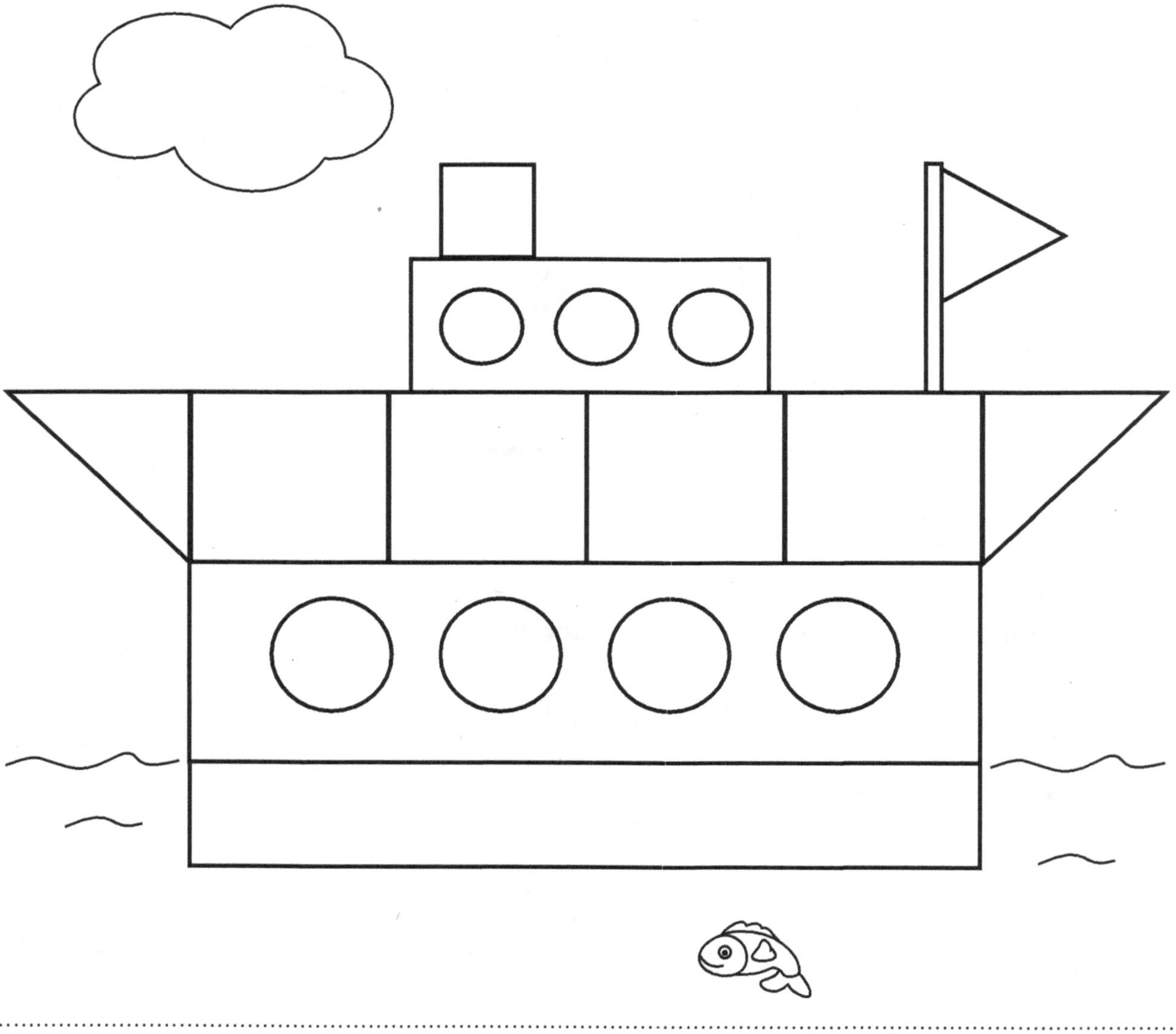

Draw circles, squares, triangles, and rectangles on sheets of colored paper. Have your child practice cutting out the shapes. Then have him or her arrange the shapes and glue them in place to make pictures.

Twinkle, Twinkle, Little Star

Listen to the nursery rhyme.

Twinkle, twinkle, little star
How I wonder what you are!
Up above the world so high.
Like a diamond in the sky.

When the blazing sun is gone,
When he nothing shines upon,
Then you show your little light,
Twinkle, twinkle, all the night.

- Traditional

Talk about it.

1. Why is the star like a diamond?
2. When does the star show its light?
3. Why do you think stars look like lights in the sky?
4. Circle the words that rhyme.

Trace and write.

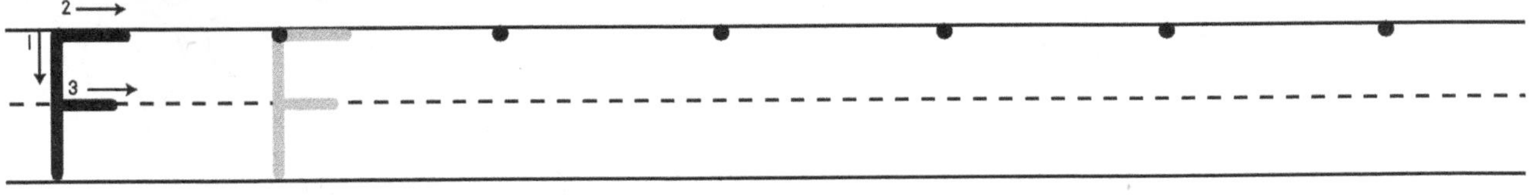

Let your child help you make star-shaped sugar cookies. Roll out the dough and have your child use a cookie cutter to make the star shape. After the cookies bake, have your child decorate them with frosting and colored sugar crystals.

Up in the Sky

Draw a line to the picture that completes each pattern.

1.

2.

3.

4.

5.

Play a pattern game using sounds with your child. Create a pattern such as *clap, stomp, clap, stomp,* and have your child copy it. Encourage your child to come up with sound patterns for you to copy too.

Rhyme Time

Look at the first picture in each row. Say its name. Color the other pictures in the row that rhyme.

1.	
2.	
3.	
4.	
5.	

Trace and write.

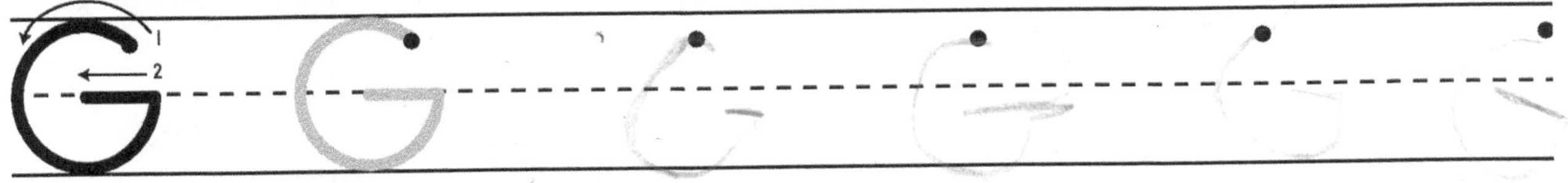

Use a black marker to draw a simple picture on a sheet of paper (example: a tree next to a lake with the sun in the sky.) Say to your child, "Color the thing that rhymes with bee." After your child colors the tree, provide another instruction that uses rhyming words (examples: cake/lake, fun/sun, my/sky). Continue until your child has colored the entire picture.

Super Shapes

Draw a line to the shape that completes each pattern.

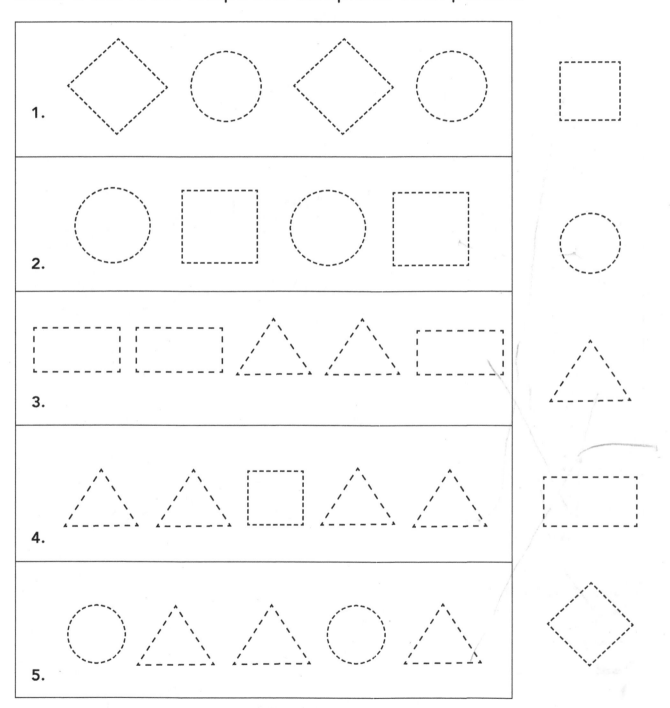

1.

2.

3.

4.

5.

Go on a pattern hunt with your child. Look at clothes, dishes, furniture, natural items, and more to see how many patterns can be identified.

Hats

Listen to the story.

Lots of people wear hats. Hats keep us warm when it is cold. Hats give us shade when it is hot. Hard hats, like helmets, keep our heads safe when we work and play. Fancy hats are worn on special days. Hats are everywhere.

Talk about it.

1. What is the story about?
2. What is a *helmet*?
3. Draw a picture of a hat that you like to wear.

Trace and write.

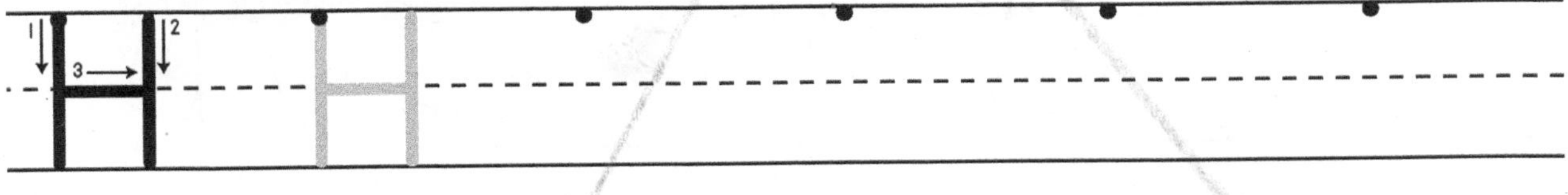

Let your child cut out pictures of people wearing hats from magazines and store catalogs. Have your child make categories for the pictures such as, cold weather hats, warm weather hats, work hats, play hats, and so on.

Pattern Power

Color the pictures to make a pattern for each row.

1.

2.

3.

4.

5.

Cut sheets of paper into two-inch wide strips. Let your child use finger paint, markers, crayons, and colored pencils to create a pattern on each strip. Staple the strips together to make a pattern book.

Catch a Match

Say the names of the pictures. Draw lines to match the rhyming words.

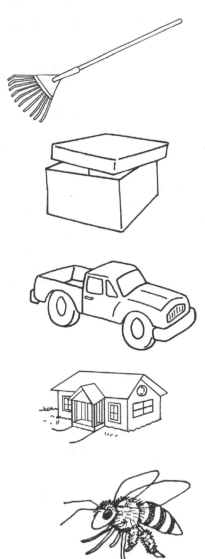

Trace and write.

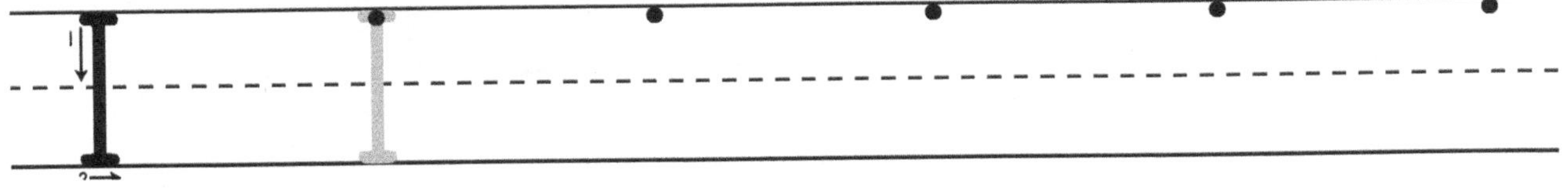

Make up nonsense words that rhyme with objects in one room of your house (examples: *dindow/window, lofa/sofa, meevee/TV, nable/table.*) Say one of the nonsense words and see if your child can find the thing in the room that rhymes with it. Continue playing until all of the objects have been identified.

Pattern Partners

Find the circles with matching patterns. Connect the dots between the matching circles to make a triangle. Use crayons to copy the pattern in each triangle that you make.

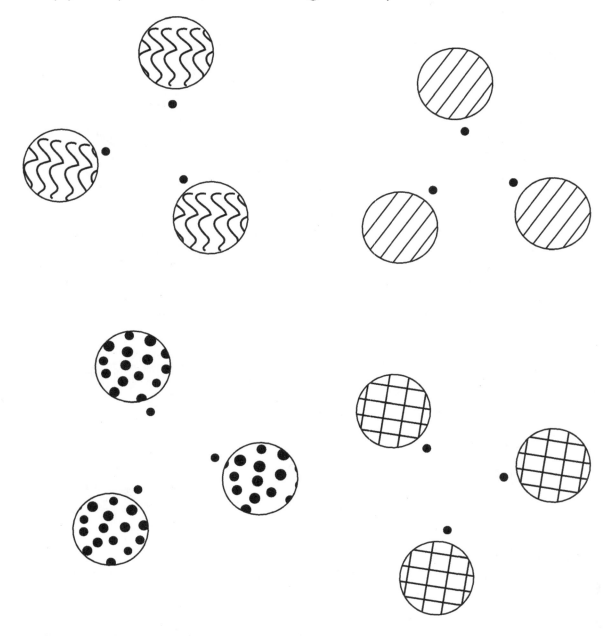

Create a movement pattern for your child to copy, such as *jump, hop, jump, hop*. Allow time to practice the movements. Then have a race from one side of a yard to the other while moving in the pattern. Take turns coming up with new movement patterns for each additional race.

Toys

Listen to the poem.

Here is the  .

doll

Here is the  .

truck

Here is the pull-along wooden  .

duck

Here is the 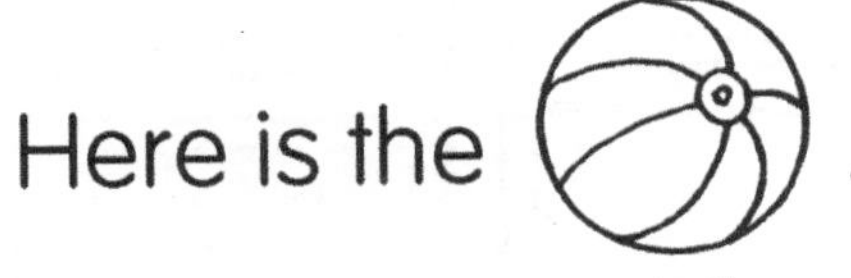 .

ball

Here is the  .

bear

Here are the toys for us to share.

Mark the words as shown in the box.

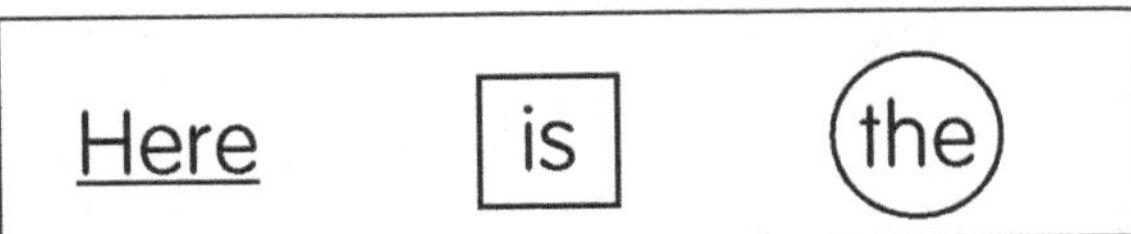

Talk about it.

1. What is the poem about?
2. Which words rhyme?
3. What are children supposed to do with these toys?
4. Practice reading the poem aloud. Touch each word as you say it.

Trace and write.

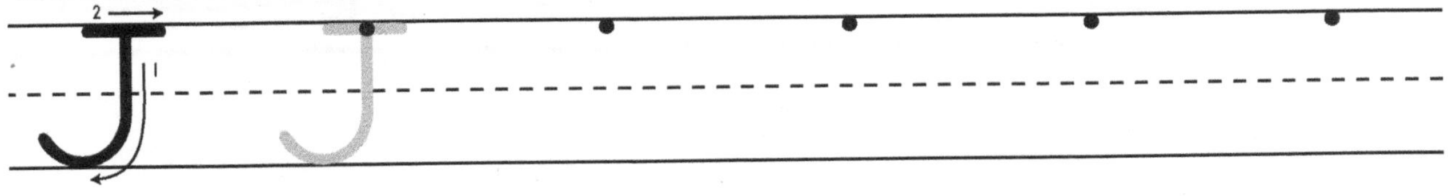

Write the words *here, is,* and *the* on separate pieces of cardboard. Have your child paint glue over the letters and cover them with glitter. Then have him or her practice reading the words.

Quilting Time

Color the quilt. Use a new color pattern for each square.

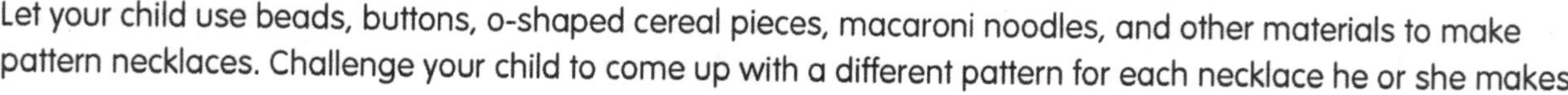

Let your child use beads, buttons, o-shaped cereal pieces, macaroni noodles, and other materials to make pattern necklaces. Challenge your child to come up with a different pattern for each necklace he or she makes.

Little Jack Horner

Listen to the nursery rhyme.

Little Jack Horner sat in a corner,
Eating a Christmas pie;
He put in his thumb, and he took out a plum,
And said, "What a good boy am I!"

- Traditional

Talk about it.

1. Who is this nursery rhyme about?
2. Why do you think he was sitting in a corner?
3. What did Jack find in his pie? Do you think that makes him a good boy?
4. Circle the words in the rhyme that start with *p*.

Trace and write.

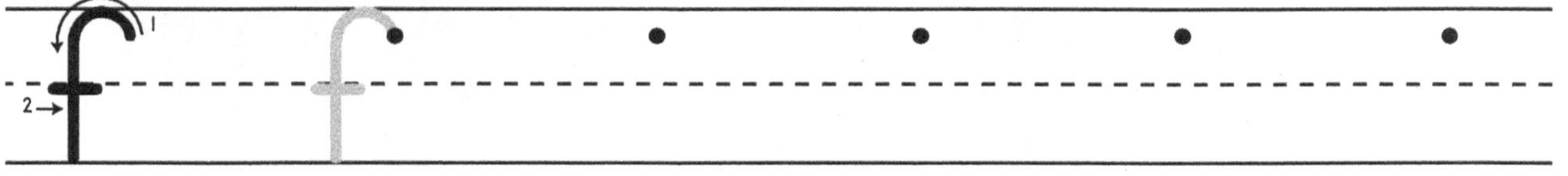

Read the rhyme aloud several times to your child. Then ask him or her to recite it with you.

Batter Up!

Underline the first picture in each row. Circle the fifth picture in each row. Color the pictures.

1.

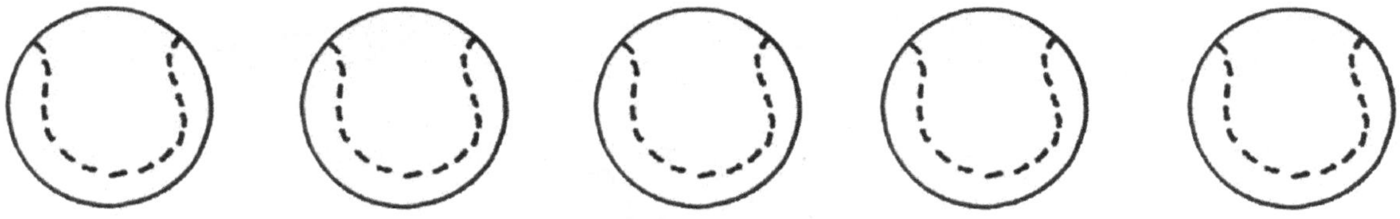

2.

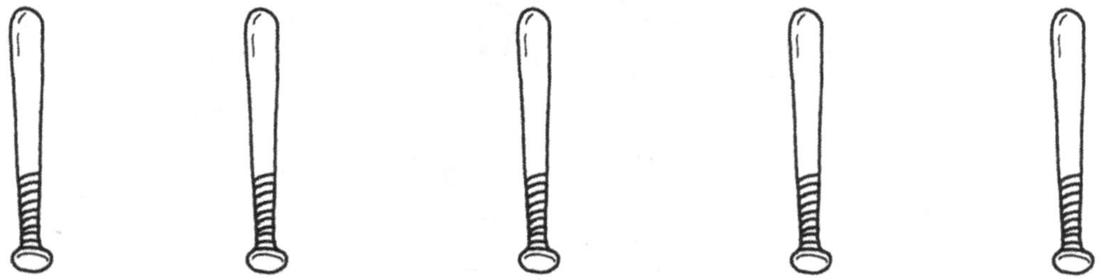

3.

4.

5.

Have your child arrange sets of toys in a line. Have him or her identify which toy is first, second, third, and so on.

P is for Pets

Say the name of each picture. Circle the letter that matches the first sound.

1. t m e	2. g s q
3. r l a	4. d z g
5. f c j	6. y i b

Trace and write.

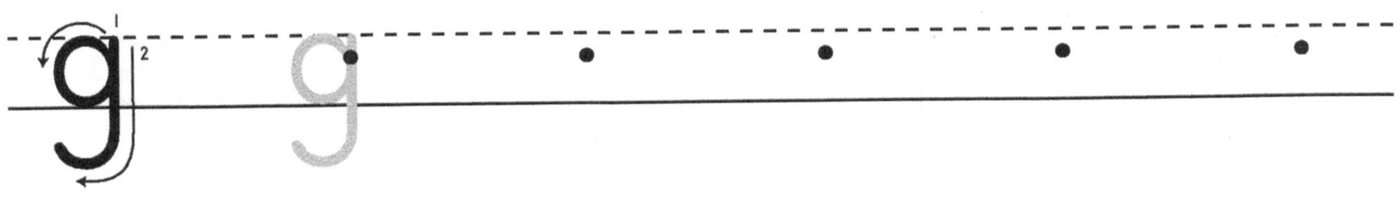

Have your child cut out pictures from old magazines, grocery flyers, and junk mail. Then have him or her sort the pictures by the first sound heard in each word.

Get the Scoop

Say the name of the number on each cone. Draw scoops of ice cream on top of the cone to match the number.

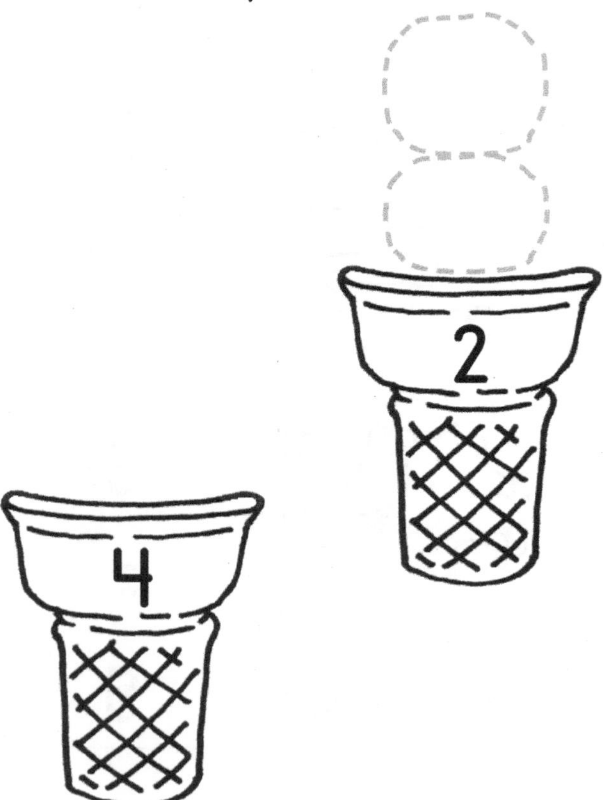

Write the numbers 1 through 10 on separate slips of paper. Have your child arrange the numbers in order from smallest to largest. Then give your child 10 chenille stems (pipe cleaners) and an assortment of pony beads. Have your child string one bead on the first stem, two beads on the second stem, three beads on the third stem, and so on. Finally, have your child match the bead stems to the numbers on the slips of paper.

Carnival Time

Look at the chart. It tells how many tickets are needed for each thing at the carnival.

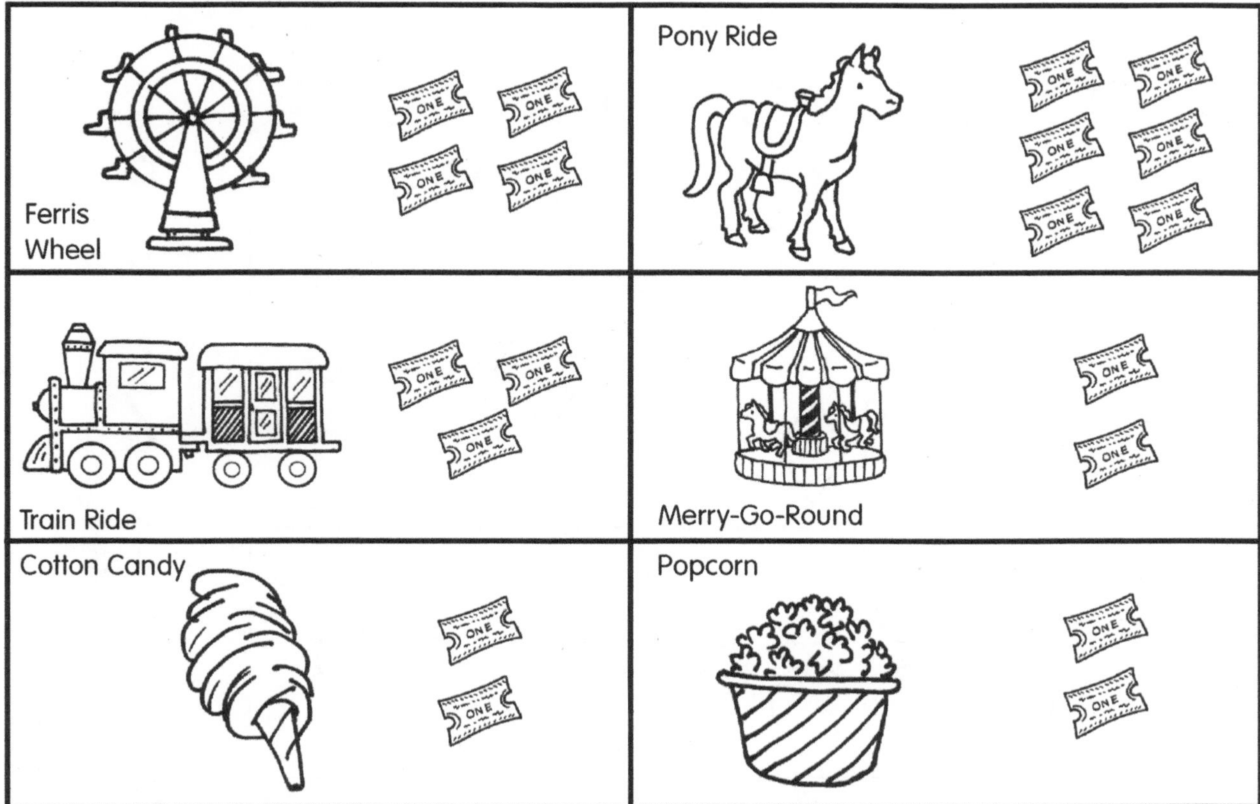

Talk about it.

1. Which ride takes the most tickets?
2. Which ride takes the least tickets?
3. How many tickets do you need for cotton candy and popcorn?
4. If you had 10 tickets, what would you use them for?

Trace and write.

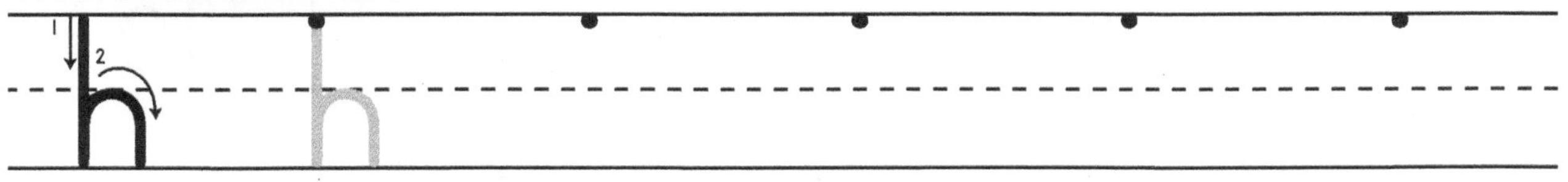

Help your child make a picture chart that shows some of his or her favorite books. Sort the books by author and write the authors' names on a sheet of poster board. Then let your child take photographs of the books written by the selected authors, print out the photos and glue them to the chart next to the appropriate author.

The More, The Merrier

Count the sets. Circle the set that shows more. Draw a line to the number that matches the circled set.

1.	(3 hearts) (7 hearts)	6
2.	(8 diamonds) (4 diamonds)	7
3.	(10 circles) (5 circles)	8
4.	(1 oval) (6 ovals)	9
5.	(9 squares) (2 squares)	10

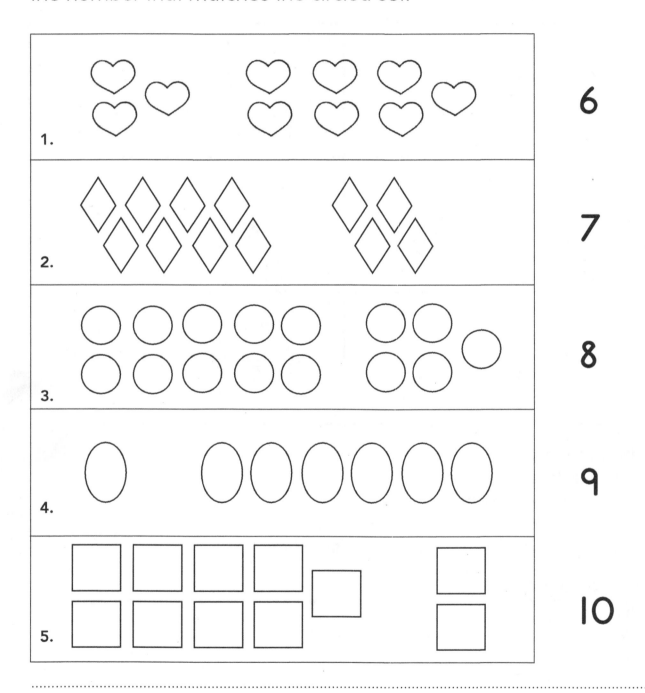

Have your child use measuring spoons to scoop out different quantities of snack foods like cereal, raisins, or crackers. Encourage your child to estimate which set of food has more and which has less. Then have him or her count the individual pieces in each set.

What Sound Do You Hear?

Color the pictures with the same beginning sound as the first picture in each row.

1.				
2.				
3.				
4.				
5.				
6.				

Trace and write.

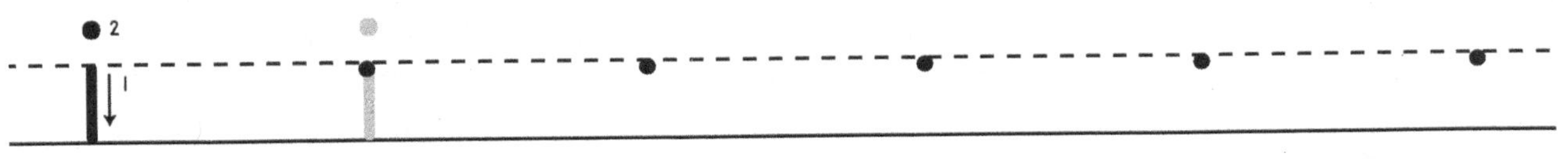

Choose a letter and see how many words you and your child can name that begin with that letter.

Tooty-Fruity

Trace the numbers. Draw a line to the matching set of fruit.

1

2

3

4

5

6

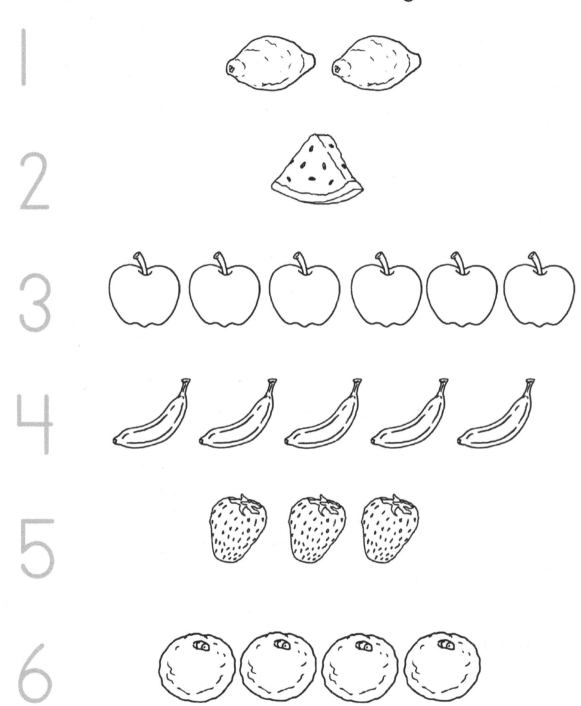

Give your child a clean paint brush and a bucket of water. Have him or her "paint" the numbers 1 to 10 on the sidewalk.

Listen to the poem.
Mark the words shown in the box.

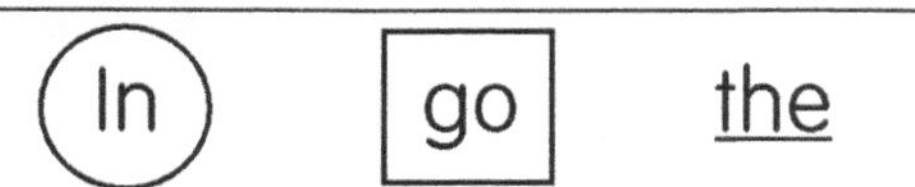

Fruit Salad

In go the  apples. In go the 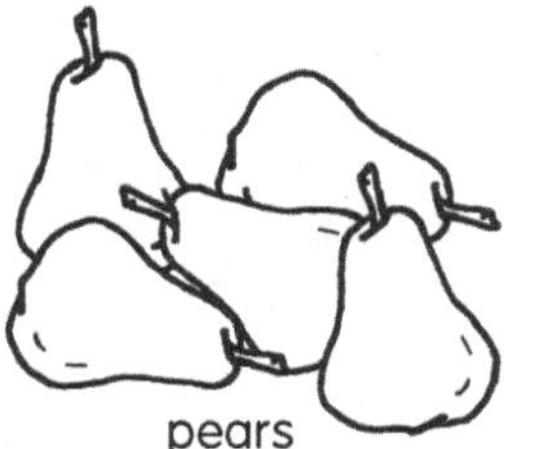 pears.

In go the  peaches. **We're almost there.**

In go the  oranges. In go the  grapes.

In go the  cherries. **Fruit salad's great!**

Talk about it.

1. What is being made in this poem?
2. What is the first fruit put in the salad? What is the last fruit?
3. Name three more fruits that can be added to the salad.
4. Practice reading the poem aloud. Touch each word as you say it.

Trace and write.

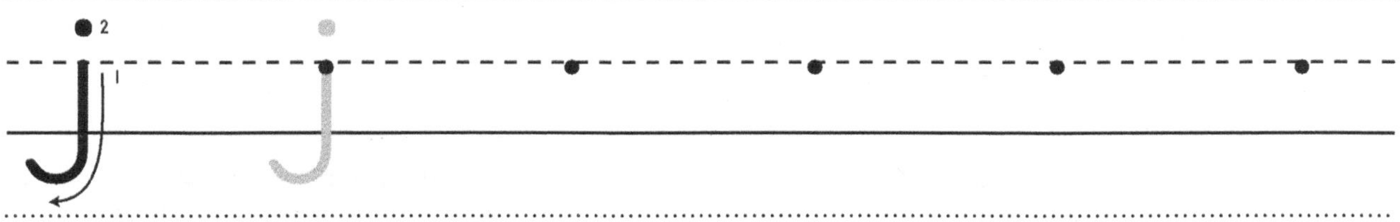

Make a fruit salad with your child. After you cut the fruit, have your child add it to the bowl in the same order as shown in the poem.

Flower Power

Count the petals on each flower. Write the number in the center.

Let your child make a number sticker book. Fold three sheets of paper in half and staple them together along the fold. On the front cover write a title such as "Sarah's Sticker Book." Let your child decorate the front and back cover. Then number the inside pages of the book in order from 1 to 10. Have your child place a matching number of stickers to each of the numbered pages.

Diddle, Diddle, Dumpling

Listen to the nursery rhyme.

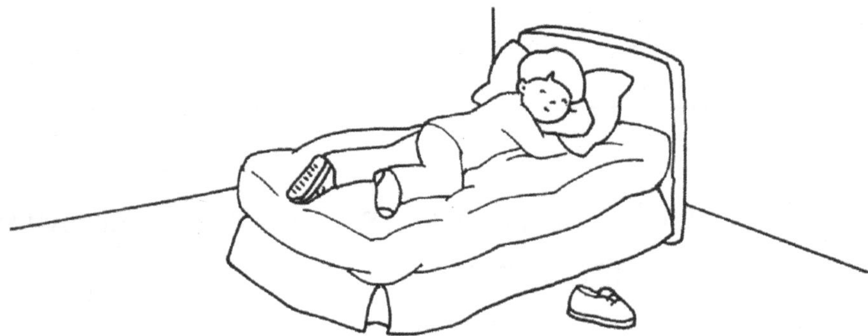

Diddle, diddle, dumpling, my son, John,
Went to bed with his trousers on;
One shoe off, and one shoe on,
Diddle, diddle, dumpling, my son, John!

- Traditional

Talk about it.

1. Who do you think is telling this story?
2. What are *trousers*?
3. Tell about a time when you wanted to sleep in your clothes rather than your pajamas.
4. Circle the words in the rhyme that start with *d*.

Trace and write.

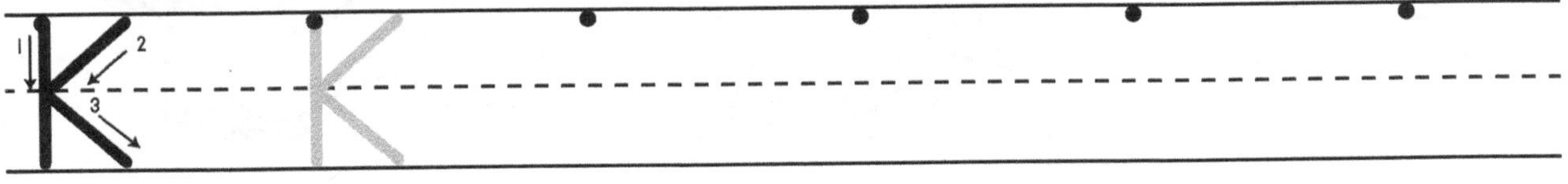

Practice the position words *on* and *off* by playing a "Simon Says" game with your child. First assemble a collection of clothing that your child can easily put on and take off independently, such as hats, socks, and jackets. Then explain the rule that the child can only follow the directions given if first you say, "Simon Says." Begin giving directions like, "Simon says put on a hat. Simon says take off your socks. Put on a jacket." If anyone puts on a jacket, that player is out because you didn't say "Simon says" first.

What's First?

Trace and write the numbers.

1 2 3

Look at the pictures. Write the numbers 1, 2, or 3 to show what happened first, second, and third.

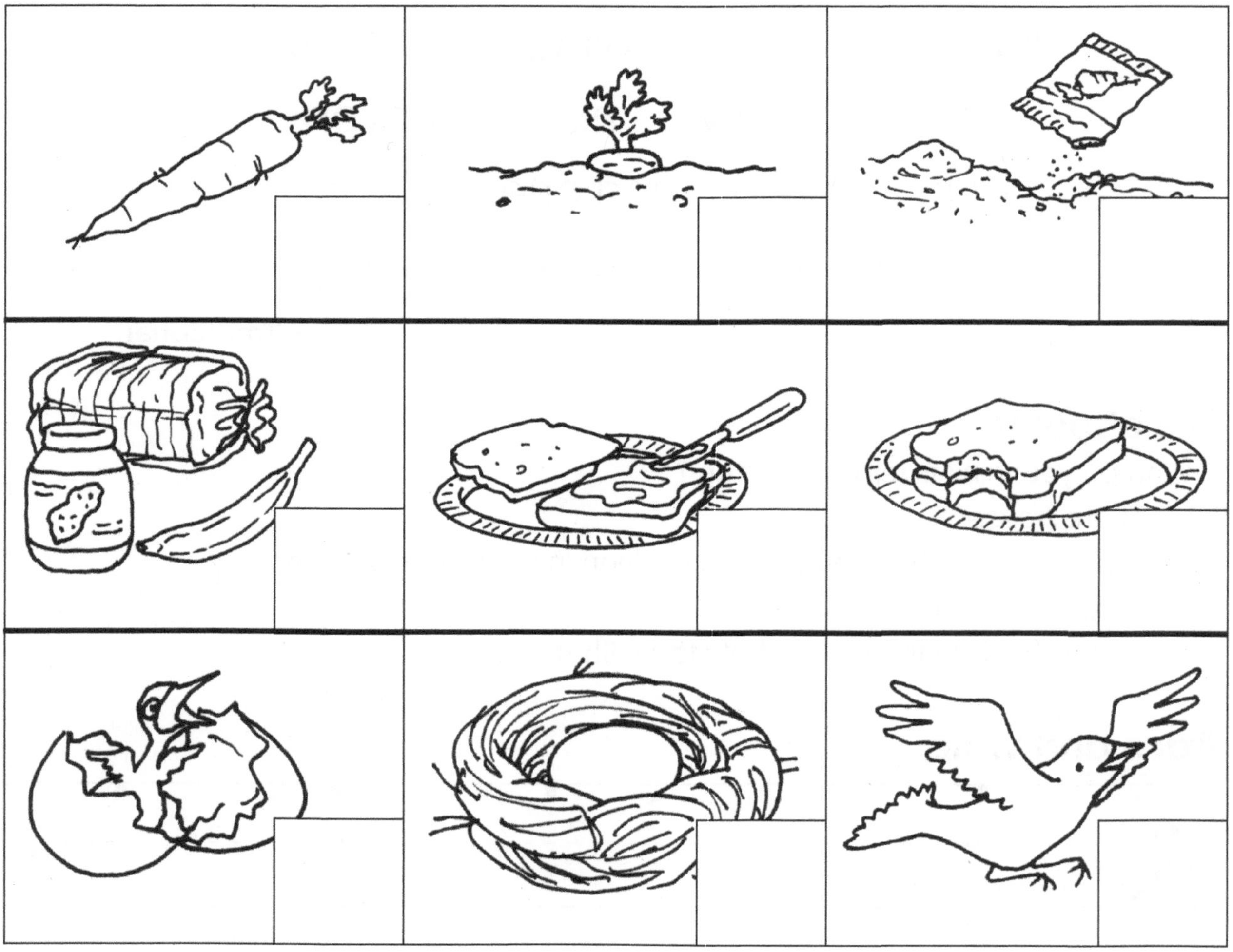

Take photographs of different members of your family completing three-step activities (examples: putting on a sock, then a shoe, and then tying the lace; putting soap on hands, then washing under water, and drying with a towel; putting on a helmet, riding a bike, and putting bike away, etc.) Print the photos, mix them up, and have your child sort them and place them in the correct sequence.

In the End

Use the code to color the shirts.

Words that end with:			
/t/	blue	/p/	yellow
/m/	red	/r/	green

Trace and write.

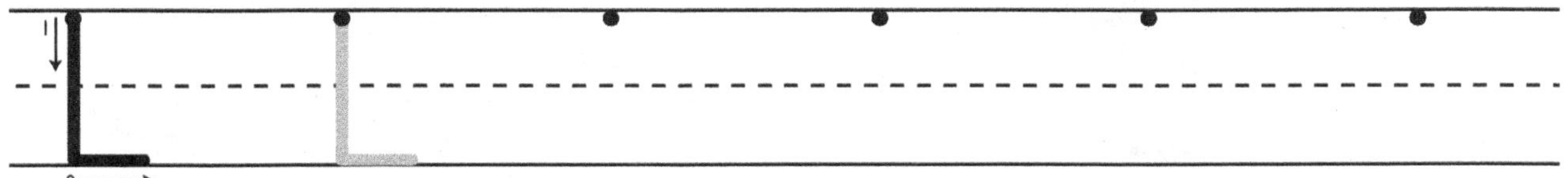

Play this game with your child to practice beginning and ending sounds. Select a toy from your child's room, such as a car. Say the word car and emphasize the/r/ sound at the end. Ask your child to find a toy that begins with the same sound that car ends with. Have your child tell you the ending sound of the toy he or she chose. Then find a toy that begins with that same sound. Continue alternating roles for as long as your child is interested in the game.

Day or Night?

Look at the pictures. Color the sun for daytime activities. Color the moon for nighttime activities.

1. 	 ☼	 ☾
2. 	 ☼	 ☾
3. 	 ☼	 ☾
4. 	 ☼	 ☾
5. 	 ☼	 ☾

Have your child decorate one side of a paper plate to look like the sun and the other side to look like the moon. Think of things your child does during a typical day or evening. Name one thing at a time and have your child hold up the plate to indicate when the activity happens—in the daytime or at night.

Puppies

Listen to the story.

There are many different kinds of puppies. Some are big. Some are small. Some have long hair. Some have short hair. Puppies can have long, floppy ears or short, stubby ears.

Puppies have many ways that they are alike too. Puppies like to play. They like to make friends. They take lots of naps. They explore every place that they go. Puppies are a lot of fun.

Talk about it.

1. How are puppies different?
2. How are puppies alike?
3. What do you think makes puppies fun?

Trace and write.

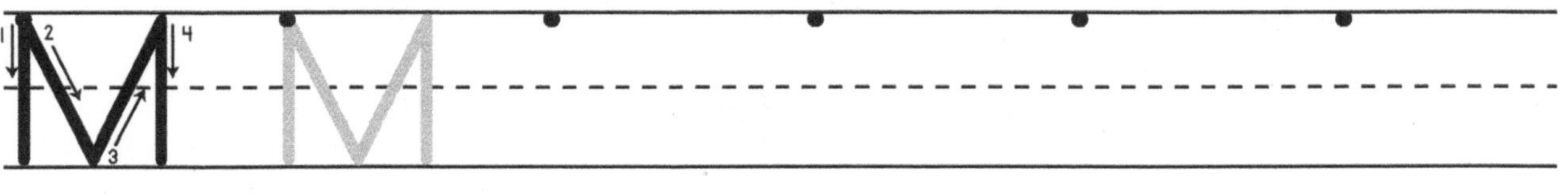

Take your child on a tour of a local animal shelter. Ask the shelter staff to talk about what puppies need to be safe and healthy. Help your child write a thank you note to the shelter afterward.

Mix-Up Fix-Up

Look at each group. Cross out the thing that does not belong.
Draw a picture in the box of something that does belong.

1. 	
2. 	
3. 	
4. 	

Have your child sort toys based on different attributes such as size, color, use and so on.

Look at a Book

Say the name of the picture on each book. Draw another picture with the same ending sound.

Trace and write.

N N

Look at an illustration from a book you are reading with your child. Have your child point out different things in the illustration and tell you the ending sound for each thing.

Over, Under

Color the picture. Use the words in the box to tell where things are.

in	on	under	over	between	beside

Play a guessing game to help your child practice using position words. Select an item in your child's room, but do not reveal what it is. Give clues such as, *It is on the bed. It is between the bear and the book. It is under the poster.* Continue providing clues until your child can identify the item. Then switch roles and see if you can guess what your child describes for you.

Listen to the poem.

Color the kites to match the color words.

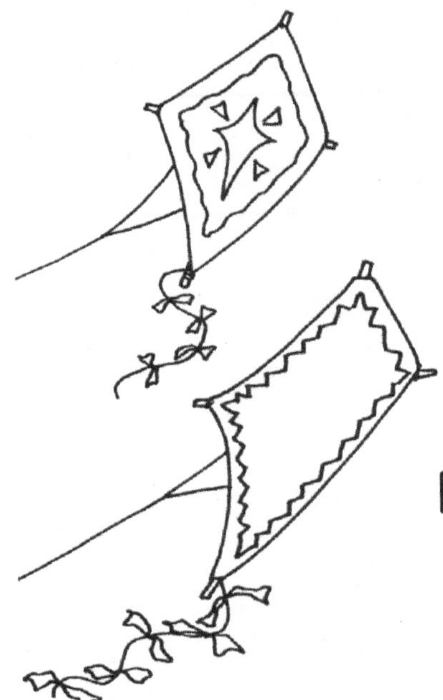

Kites

Blue kite,
Green kite,
Yellow kite,
Red.
Kites flying in the sky,
Way up overhead.

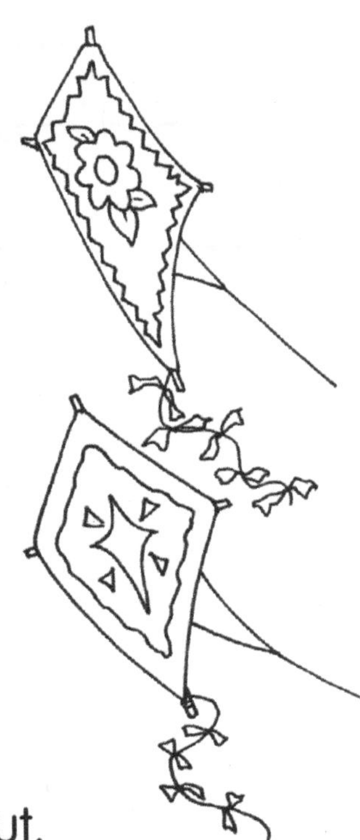

Draw a picture that shows what this poem is about.

Trace and write.

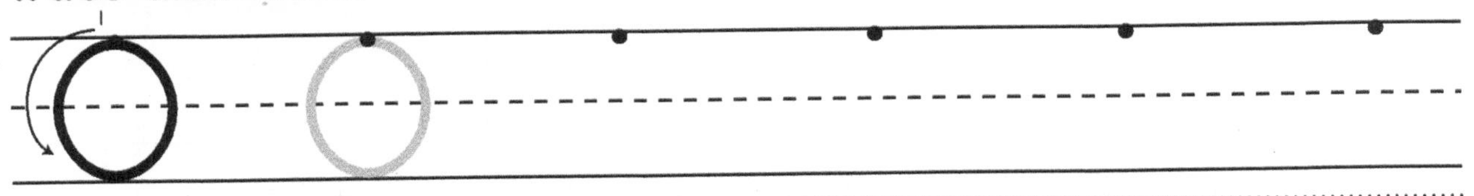

Write color words on various slips of paper. Let your child use the paper slips to label the colors of different things around the house.

A Rainbow of Colors

Trace the words. Draw pictures of things for each color.

red	orange	yellow
blue	green	purple

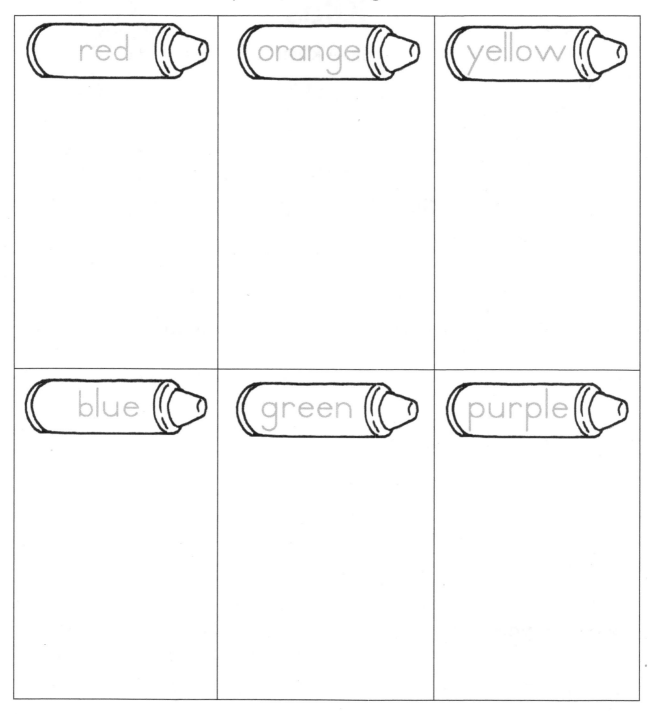

Using finger paints is a great way for children to experiment with colors. Provide lots of paint and paper and celebrate the masterpieces that are created!

One, Two, Buckle My Shoe

Listen to the nursery rhyme.

One, two, buckle my shoe;
Three, four, shut the door;
Five, six, pick up sticks;
Seven, eight, lay them straight;
Nine, ten, a good fat hen.

- Traditional

Talk about it.

1. What happens first in the rhyme?
2. What is supposed to be laid straight?
3. There is an action that happens in each line, except the last one. What do you think the action should be for the "good fat hen?"
4. Circle the words that rhyme in each line.

Trace and write.

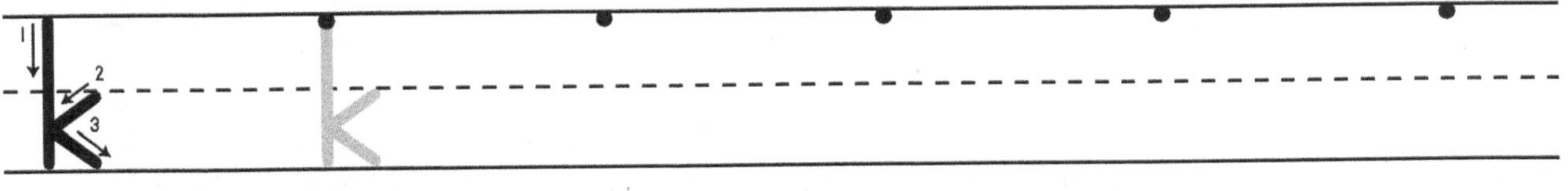

Help your child come up with different rhyming words for the numbers *two, four, six, eight,* and *ten*. Then see if together you can make a new nursery rhyme. For example, "One, two, color me blue; Three, four, sweep the floor."

Beautiful Butterflies

Trace and write the numbers.

1 1 1

2 2 2

3 3 3

4 4 4

Count the butterflies. Write the number.

Make a simple memory match game for your child to practice identifying and counting numbers 0 to 4. Use 10 index cards. Number five of the cards from 0 to 4. Put stamps or stickers on the other five cards to show the quantities of 0 to 4. Shuffle the cards and place them face down on a table. Take turns with your child, flipping two cards over at a time until a matching pair is found. Continue playing until all the matches have been found.

Fishing for Vowels

Say the name of each picture in the box. Point to the letter in the word that makes the short vowel sound.

Color the fish that have short vowel words.
Cross out the fish that do not.

Trace and write.

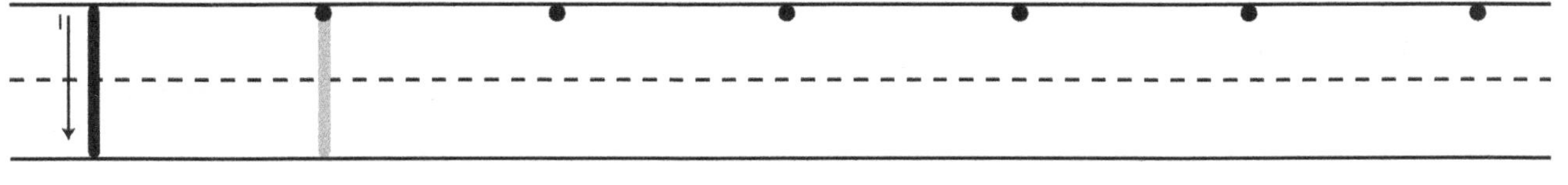

Help your child distinguish the number of sounds in one-syllable words. Say the word *cat*. Then clap your hands one time for each individual sound in the word (/*c*/, clap; /*a*/, clap; /*t*/, clap). At the end, clap your hands one more time as you put all the sounds together again to say the word (*cat*, clap). Use the words on this page for more practice.

Lovely Ladies

Trace and write the numbers.

5 5 5

6 6 6

7 7 7

8 8 8

Count the ladybugs. Write the number.

Help your child make paper-chain caterpillars to practice counting. Cut colored paper into 2" x 6" strips. Roll one strip of paper into a loop and glue the ends together. Then put the next strip of paper through the loop and glue the ends together so that two loops are connected. Continue adding more loops to make the caterpillar. Have your child count the total number of loops on the caterpillar and write the number on the last piece. Make caterpillars of different lengths to practice numbers to 8.

The Amazing Body

Listen to the story.

Your body has amazing parts that help you experience the world. You use your eyes to see. You use your ears to hear. Look outside. See the trees. Hear the birds. Your nose and mouth help you too. You use your nose to smell. You use your mouth to taste. Go in your kitchen. What do you smell? What can you taste? Even your skin helps you. Your skin helps you feel things. Rub a feather on your arm. That tickles! Now try to use your eyes, ears, nose, mouth, and skin all at the same time! Isn't the body amazing?

Talk about it.

1. What parts of the body help you experience the world?
2. What parts of your body help you to see and hear?
3. What parts help you smell, taste, and feel?

Draw a picture to show how you can use your eyes, ears, nose, mouth, and skin all at the same time.

Trace and write.

m m

Have a tasting party with your child. Set out some healthy snacks. Have your child describe how the different foods look, sound, smell, taste, and feel. For example, popcorn looks bumpy, sounds crunchy, smells buttery, tastes salty, and feels warm.

Catch a Caterpillar

Trace and write the numbers.

9 9 9

10 10 10

11 11 11

12 12 12

Count the caterpillars. Write the number.

Number the cups in an egg carton from 1 to 12. Have your child place one dried bean in cup number 1. Then have your child roll a pair of dice, add the numbers, and fill the matching cup with the same number of dried beans. If your child rolls a number more than one time, have him or her count the beans that are already in the corresponding cup, without adding more beans. Continue playing until all 12 cups have been filled.

Matching Shoes

Color the pictures. Draw lines to match the pictures with the same long vowel sounds.

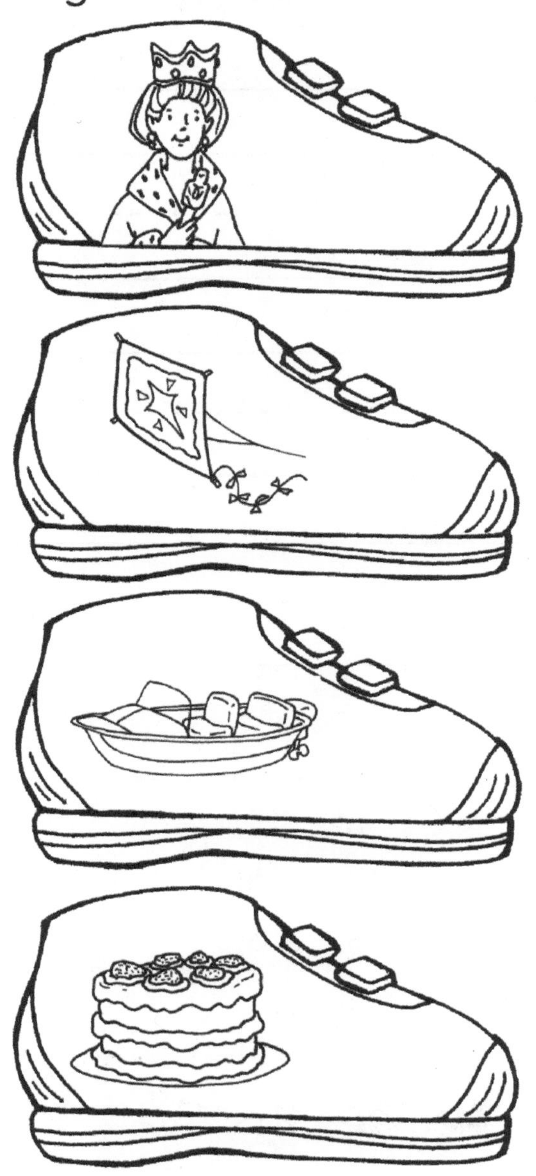

Trace and write.

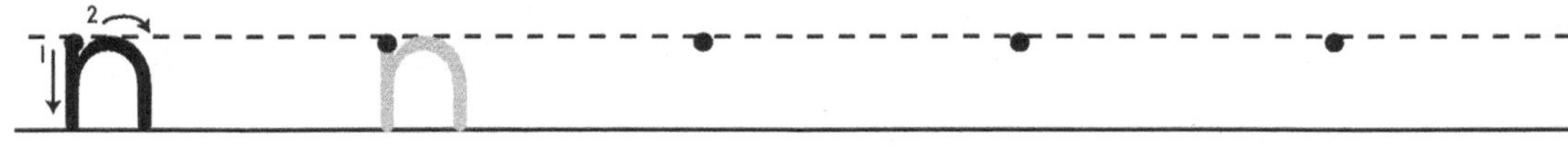

Give your child a grocery store flyer and five different colored markers. Have your child find the five vowels (a, e, i, o, u) in the flyer and color each one a different color.

The Ants Go Marching

Trace and write the numbers.

13 13 13

14 14 14

15 15 15

16 16 16

Count the ants. Write the number.

Press your child's thumb into an inkpad and then onto a sheet of paper. Repeat until you have 16 thumbprints. Have your child draw a face, two antenna, and six legs on each thumbprint to turn them into ants. Then have your child practice counting to 16, touching each ant and saying the corresponding number out loud.

Surprise!

Listen to the poem.

One, two, three, four,
Knock-knock on the door.
Five, six, seven, eight,
Shh-Shh! Hide and wait.
Nine, ten . . .
Surprise! Happy Birthday, Hen!

Talk about it.

1. What is happening in this poem?
2. Who do you think might be there?
3. Why do you think they are being told to hide?
4. Whose birthday is it?
5. Circle all the number words. Say each number's name as you go.

Trace and write.

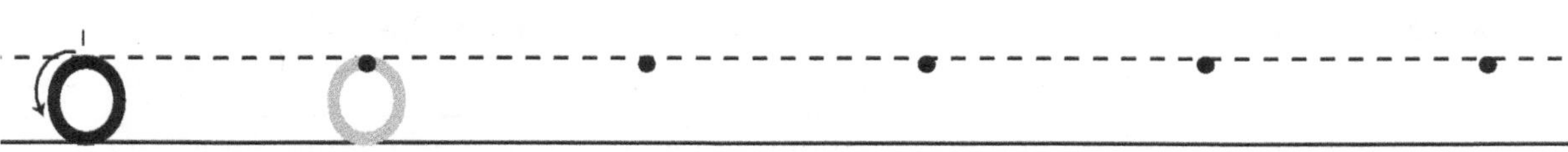

Make a simple matching puzzle for your child. Write *one* on the left side of an index card and make one dot on the right side. Do the same for the numbers *two* through *ten*. Then cut the index cards in half, making a different cut line on each card. Mix the cards up and have your child find the matches.

Munch, Munch!

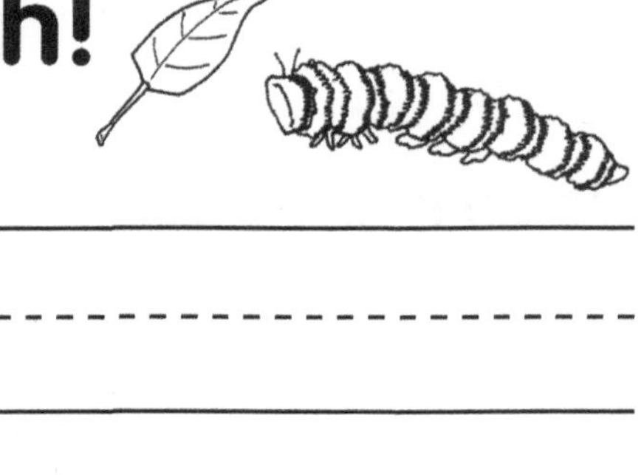

Trace and write the numbers.

17 17 17

18 18 18

19 19 19

20 20 20

Count the dots. Write the number.

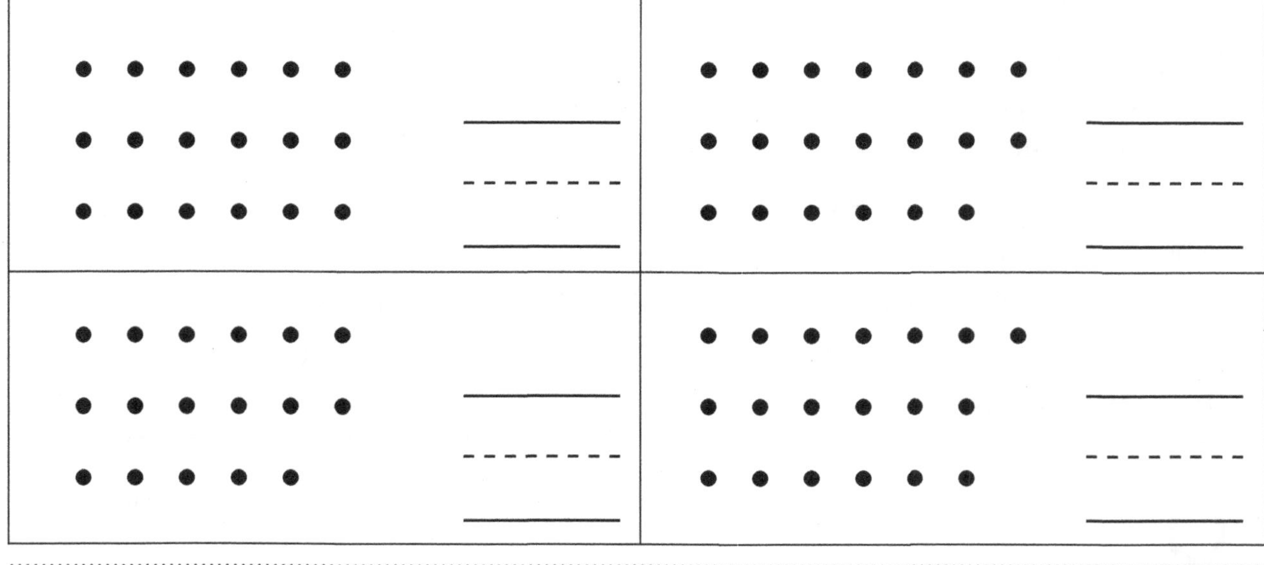

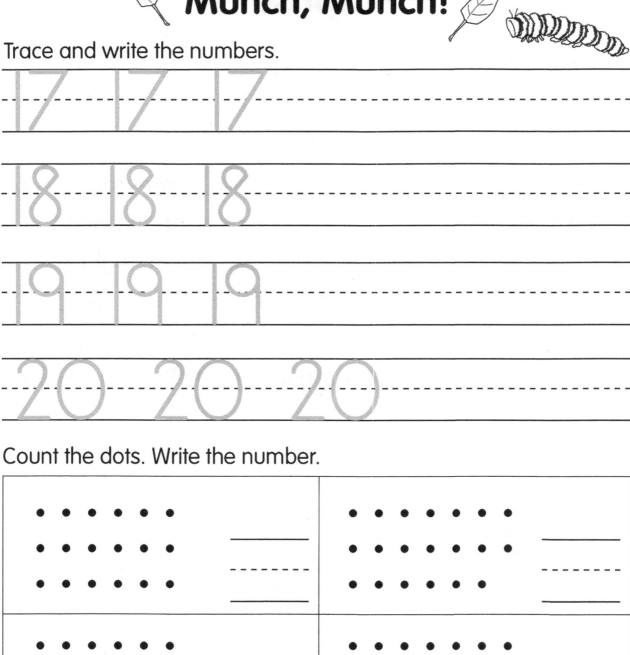

Have your child go outside and take 20 "baby steps." Use chalk to mark where the last step ends. Then have him or her go back to the starting place and take 20 "giant steps." Mark where the last step ends and have your child compare the difference between the two distances. Have your child continue finding other ways to move ahead 20 paces using different movements such as hops, jumps, and skips.

Little Boy Blue

Listen to the nursery rhyme.

Little Boy Blue, come blow your horn.
The sheep's in the meadow, the cow's in the corn.
Where is that boy who looks after the sheep?
Under the haystack, fast asleep.

- Traditional

Talk about it.

1. What is Little Boy Blue's job?
2. Why are the sheep in the meadow?
3. Where is Little Boy Blue?
4. Circle the words in the rhyme that start with *b* or *c*.

Trace and write.

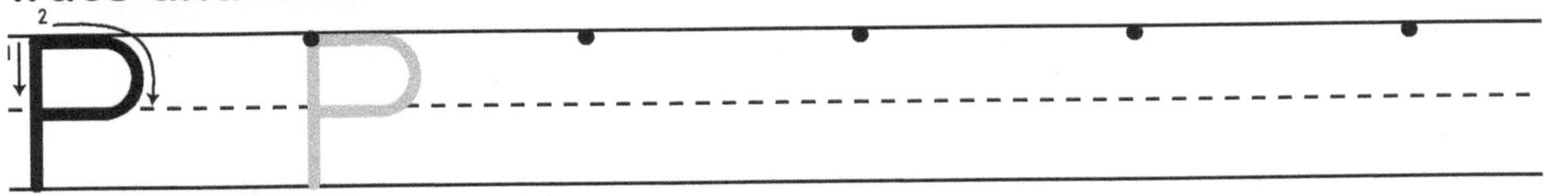

In this rhyme, Little Boy Blue falls asleep instead of doing his job. Talk with your child about jobs that he or she can help with around the house. Make a simple chore chart together and put a sticker on the chart for each chore your child completes.

Time for School

Count the objects. Write the numbers. Find the sum.

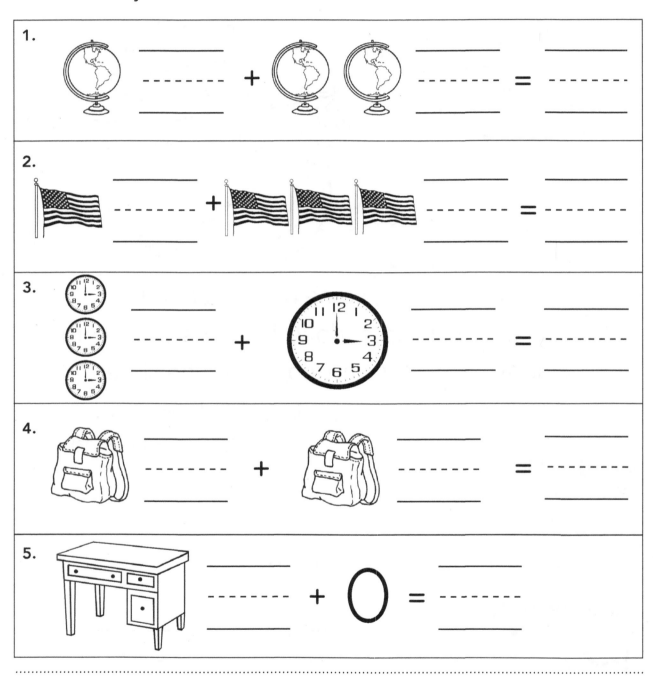

1.  _____ + _____ = _____

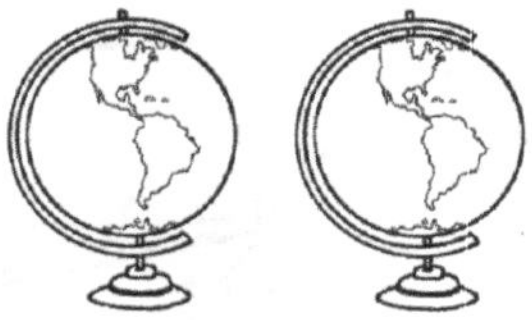

2.  _____ + _____ = _____

3.  _____ + _____ = _____

4.  _____ + _____ = _____

5.  _____ + 0 = _____

Divide a sheet of paper into even rows. Draw a plus sign and an equal sign in each row. Give your child two die, a bowl of cereal, and a bottle of glue. Have your child roll the dice, count out the number of cereal pieces for each number rolled, and glue the corresponding number of cereal pieces to either side of the plus sign. Have your child count to add the two numbers together and write the answer after the equal sign. Continue until each row is completed.

Naming Words

A noun is a word that names a person, place, or thing. Circle the nouns that name people. Underline the nouns that name places. Draw a box around the nouns that name things.

Draw pictures of nouns.

Person	Place	Thing

Trace and write.

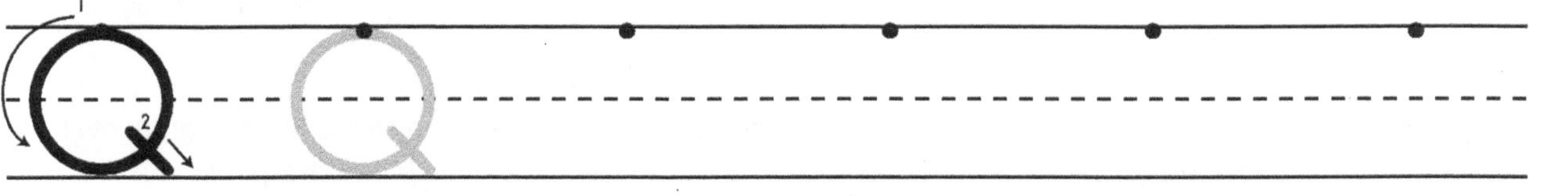

Help your child make a "Noun Notebook." Collect pictures of people, places, and things that are meaningful to your child. Have your child glue the pictures into a notebook and help him or her label each one.

One More

Count the shapes. Draw one more. Find the sum.

1.	2.
____ + ____ = ____	____ + ____ = ____
3.	4.
____ + ____ = ____	____ + ____ = ____
5.	6.
____ + ____ = ____	____ + ____ = ____

Cut about a three-foot length of yarn. Number a set of index cards from 0 to 10 and staple them in order evenly across the yarn. Stretch the yarn out and tape the ends to a wall or sidewalk. Attach a clothespin to one of the numbers. Have your child say the name of the number and then say, "Plus one." Then have your child move the clothespin one number over to show the answer to the equation. After your child is proficient with adding one, you can modify this game to practice subtracting one.

Our Neighborhood

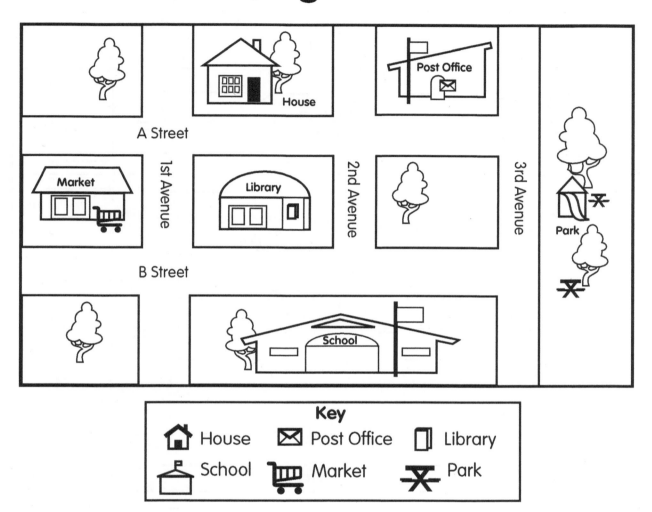

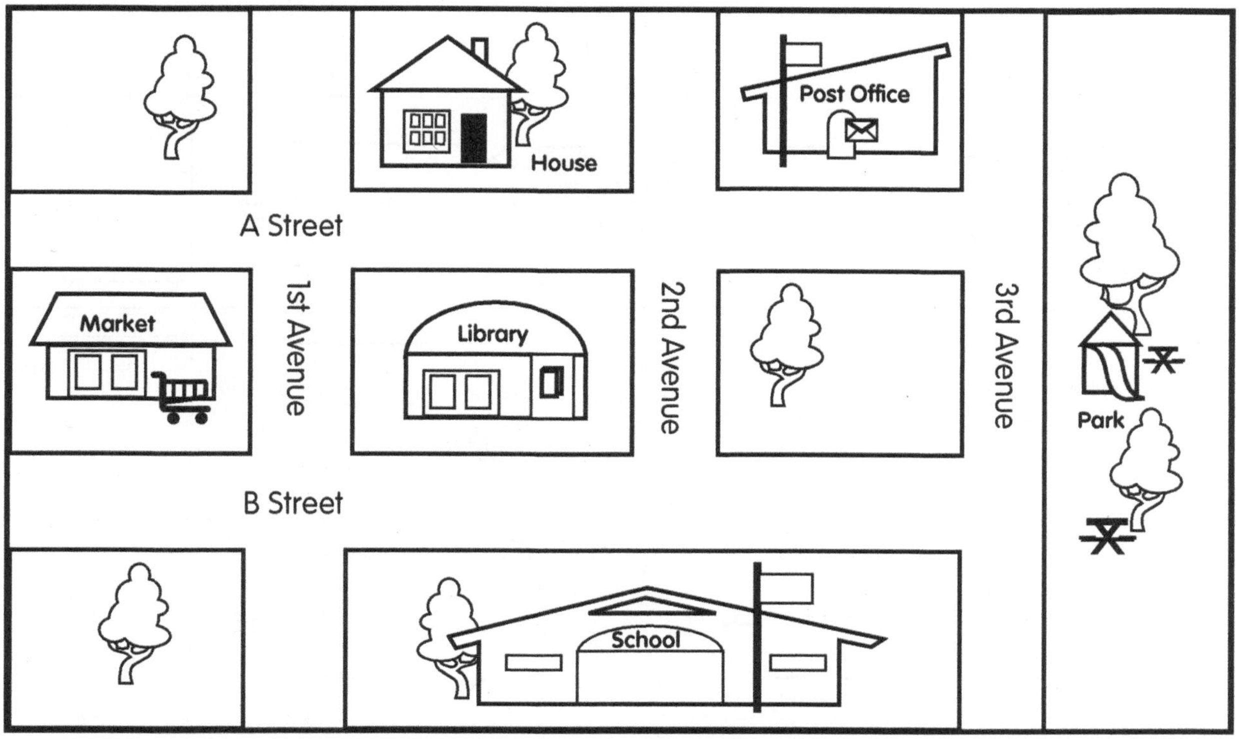

House
Post Office
A Street
Market
1st Avenue
Library
2nd Avenue
3rd Avenue
Park
B Street
School

Key

- House
- Post Office
- Library
- School
- Market
- Park

Follow the directions.

1. Use a red crayon. Draw a path from the to the .
2. Use a blue crayon. Draw a path from the to the .
3. Use a green crayon. Draw a path from the to the .

Trace and write.

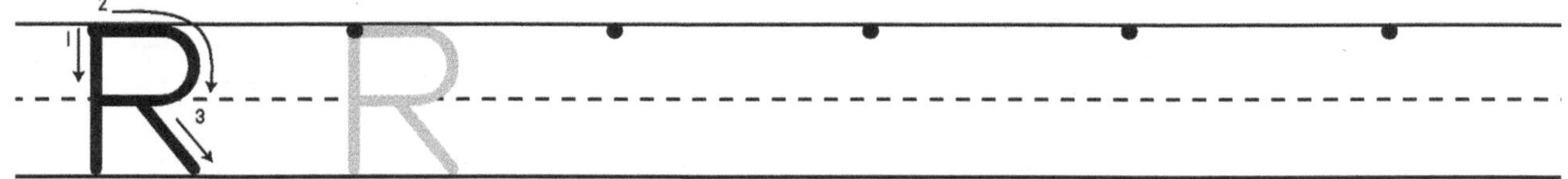

Collect old food boxes. Cover them with plain wrapping paper and let your child decorate them to look like places around your community. Then help your child set up the boxes to make a three-dimensional map of your neighborhood.

Double Up

Add.

1. 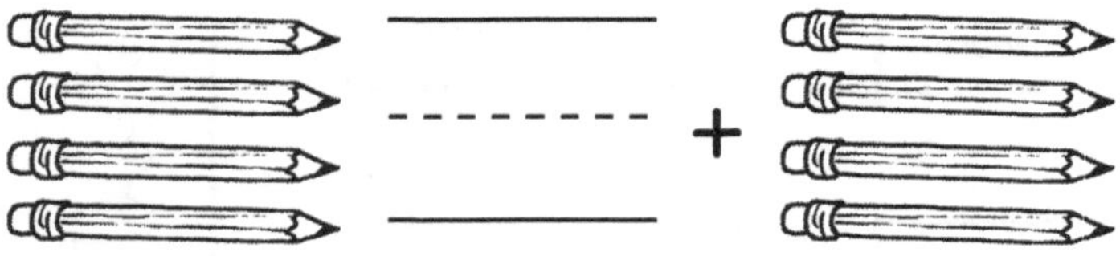 ____ + ____ =

2. 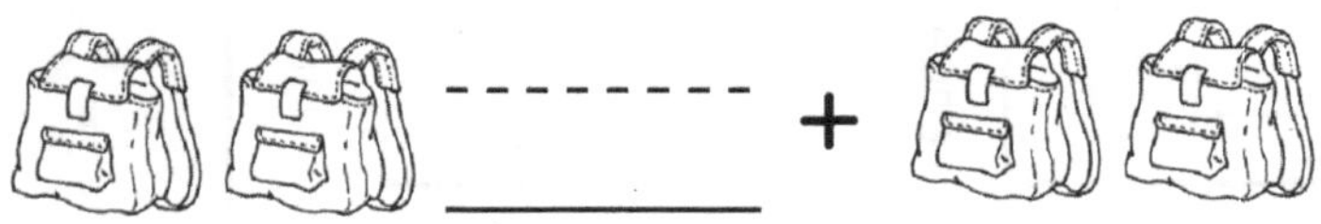 ____ + ____ =

3. 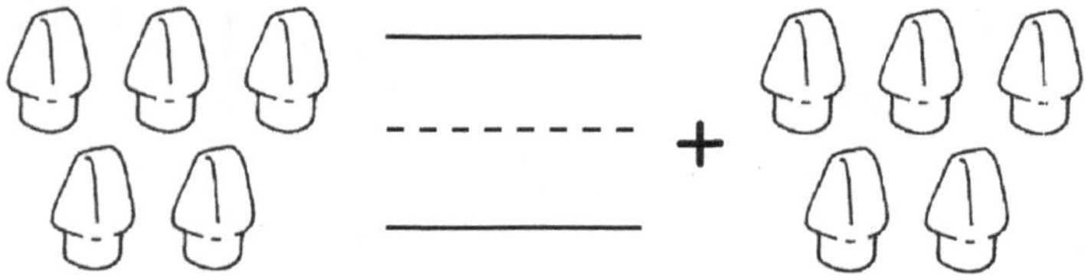 ____ + ____ =

4. 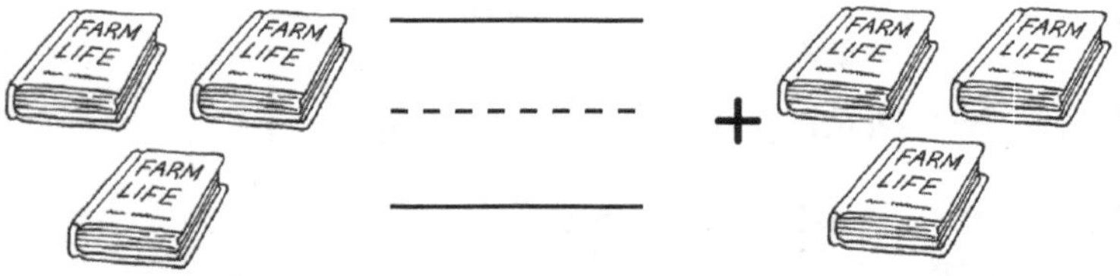 ____ + ____ =

5. 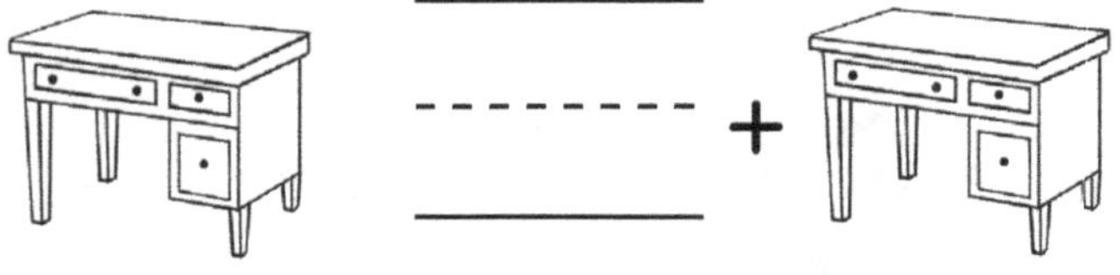 ____ + ____ =

6. 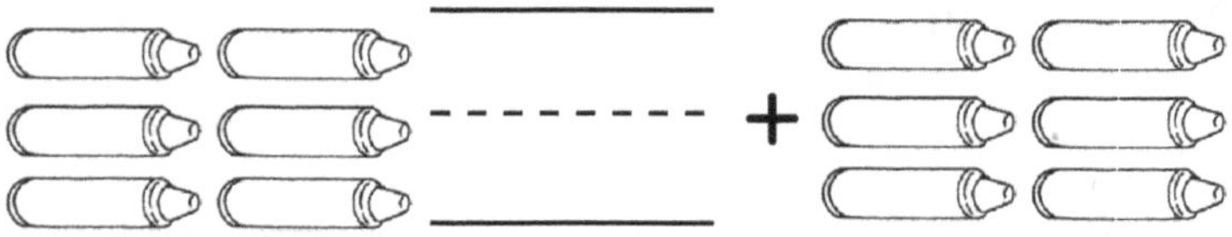 ____ + ____ =

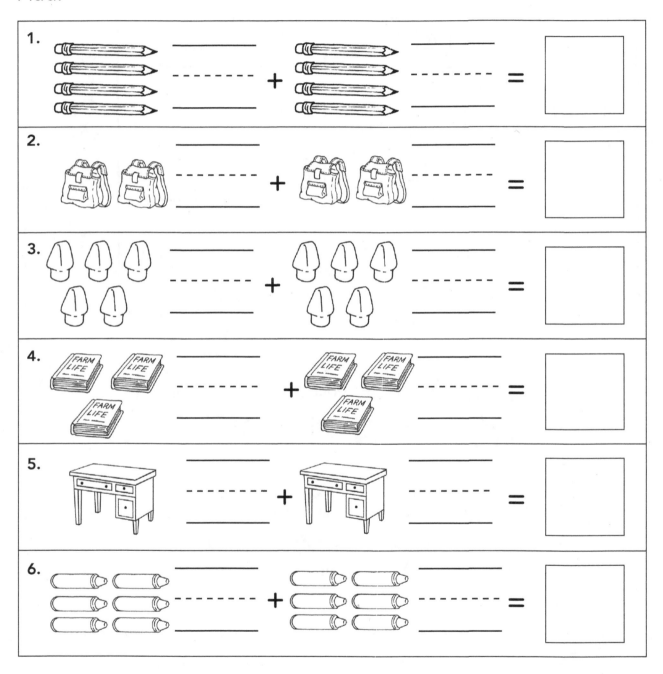

Play this game to practice adding doubles: Make a chart that shows the numbers 1 to 100. Place a red bean on each even number and a black bean on each odd number. Each player chooses a color and takes turns rolling a single die. The number that is rolled is doubled and the player removes that number of his or her beans from the board. The first player to remove all the beans wins the game.

Just Add S

A noun that describes more than one thing is a plural noun. Most nouns can be made plural just by adding an *s* to the end.

Say the name of each noun. Add *s* to make it plural. Trace the words.

1. flower flowers	2. apple apples
3. bee bees	4. heart hearts

Trace and write.

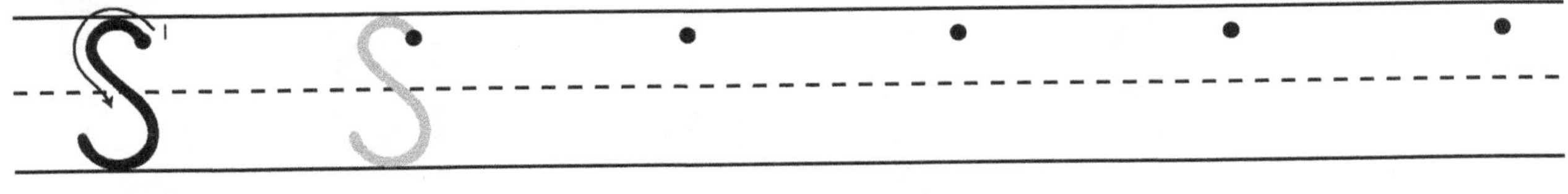

Cut the shape of a letter s from a sponge, or buy letter-shaped sponges at a craft store. Then stamp index cards with pictures, showing one picture on some cards and more than one of the same picture on other cards. To indicate a plural noun, have your child stamp the letter s sponge on the cards that show more than one.

Apple Baskets

Write a different addition problem on each apple. The sum should equal the number shown on the basket.

7
+ 0

5
+ 2

7

8

9

10

Cut an apple in half. Let your child dip the apple in paint to make apple prints. Challenge your child to show different pairs of numbers that equal the same sum. For example, to make 6, your child can make apple prints using the following pairs of numbers: 0 and 6, 1 and 5, 2 and 4, and 3 and 3.

Listen to the poem.

Monkeys

Monkeys, monkeys
In a row.
Monkeys, monkeys
High and low.
Monkeys, monkeys
In a tree.
Monkeys, monkeys
Wave at me!

Talk about it.

1. Where are the monkeys?
2. What words tell you about their places in the tree?
3. What are the monkeys doing?
4. Circle the words that rhyme.

Trace and write.

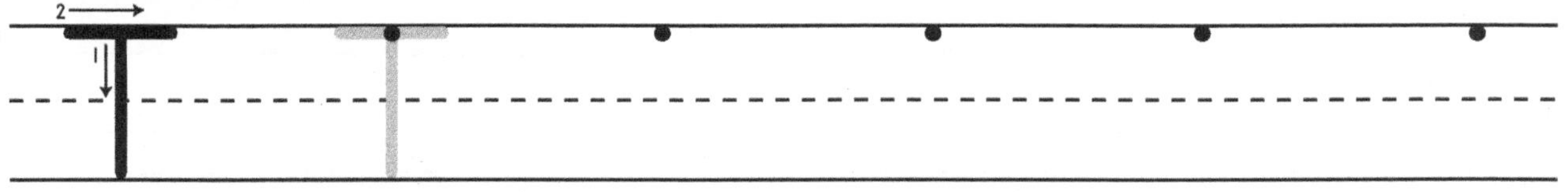

This poem uses the opposite words *high* and *low*. Have your child act out what those words mean. Then see if he or she can come up with other pairs of opposites to act out. Some examples are: *on* and *off*, *awake* and *asleep*, *big* and *little*, and *in* and *out*.

Hang Ten

Count the surfboards. Draw more to make 10.
Write the number sentence.

1. 6 + ___ = 10

2. 3 + ___ = 10

3. 5 + ___ = 10

4. 7 + ___ = 10

5. 4 + ___ = 10

Have your child use pennies to show different ways to make quantities of 10. For each set of 10 pennies, show your child a dime. Tell your child that 10 pennies has the same value as 1 dime.

Once I Saw a Little Bird

Listen to the nursery rhyme.

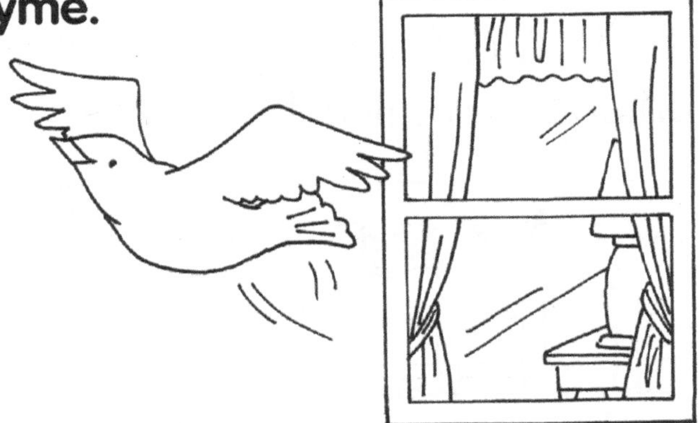

Once I saw a little bird
Come hop, hop, hop;
So I cried, "Little bird,
Will you stop, stop, stop?"
And was going to the window,
To say, "How do you do?"
But he shook his little tail,
And far away he flew.

- Traditional

Talk about it.

1. Where do you think the person was when the bird was seen?
2. What did the person want the bird to do?
3. Why do you think the bird flew away?
4. Say as many words as you can that rhyme with *hop* and *stop*.

Trace and write.

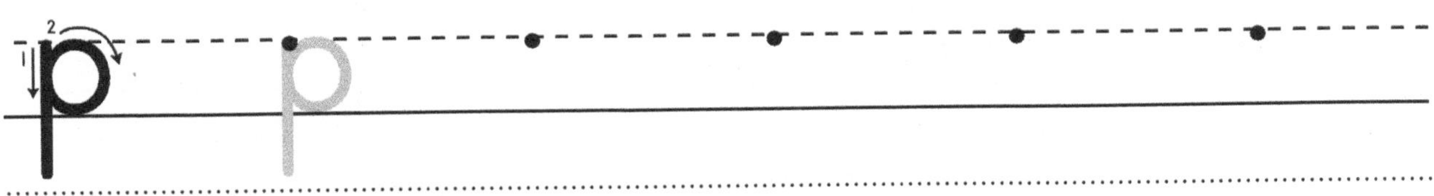

Have your child act out the nursery rhyme as you read it aloud.

Tweety-Tweet

Count the birds. Cross out the birds that are flying away. Write a number sentence to match the picture.

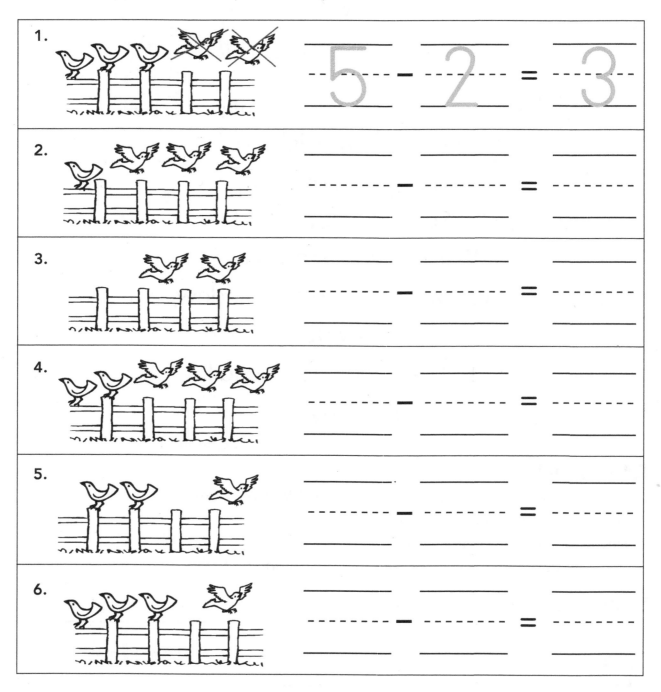

1.	5 - 2 = 3
2.	___ - ___ = ___
3.	___ - ___ = ___
4.	___ - ___ = ___
5.	___ - ___ = ___
6.	___ - ___ = ___

Draw four circles on a page. Let your child place up to 5 stickers in each circle. Have your child cross out some of the stickers and write the matching number sentence for each circle.

Action!

Verbs are action words. They tell what someone or something does. Write the verb for each picture.

run	jump	sing	sleep	read	swim

1.

2.

3.

4.

5.

6.

Trace and write.

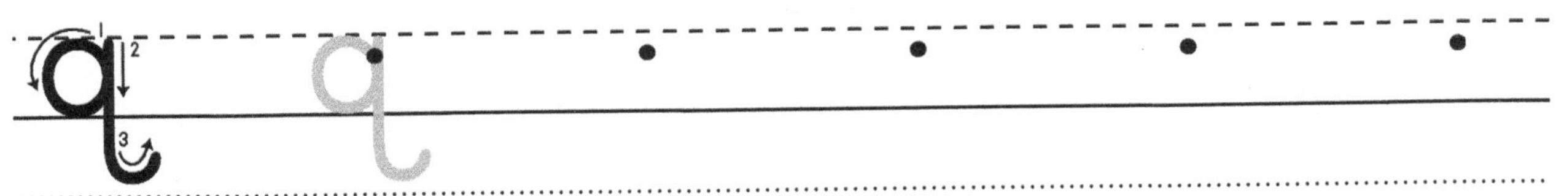

Play charades with your child using only verbs. Have one player act out a verb while the other player tries to guess what it is.

Down the Lines

Subtract 1. Use the number lines to help.

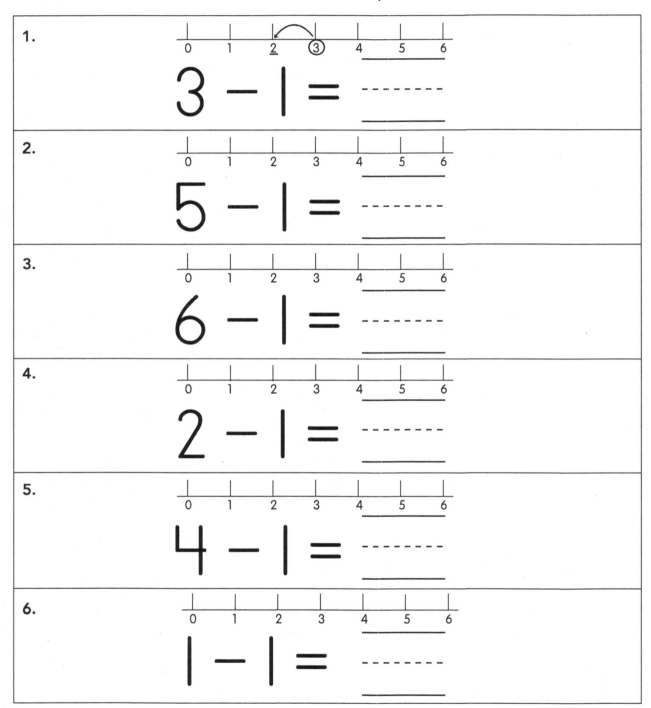

1. 0 1 2 3 4 5 6

$3 - 1 =$ ______

2. 0 1 2 3 4 5 6

$5 - 1 =$ ______

3. 0 1 2 3 4 5 6

$6 - 1 =$ ______

4. 0 1 2 3 4 5 6

$2 - 1 =$ ______

5. 0 1 2 3 4 5 6

$4 - 1 =$ ______

6. 0 1 2 3 4 5 6

$1 - 1 =$ ______

Give your child a pair of dice. Have him or her roll the dice and add the two numbers together. Then ask him to tell you what is left if you subtract one from the sum.

Pets

Listen to the story.

Many people enjoy keeping pets. Some pets, like dogs and cats, need lots of attention. They need to be played with, have their fur brushed, and get lots of exercise. Other pets, like turtles and fish, need less attention but they still need to be taken care of. When you have a pet, you have to make sure that they get food and water every day. You have to make sure your pets are healthy and safe. Pets are a lot of responsibility, but they make lots of people happy.

Talk about it.

1. What is this story about?
2. What are some of the things a pet dog needs?
3. What needs more attention, a cat or a turtle?
4. Tell about a pet you have or one you would like to have.

Trace and write.

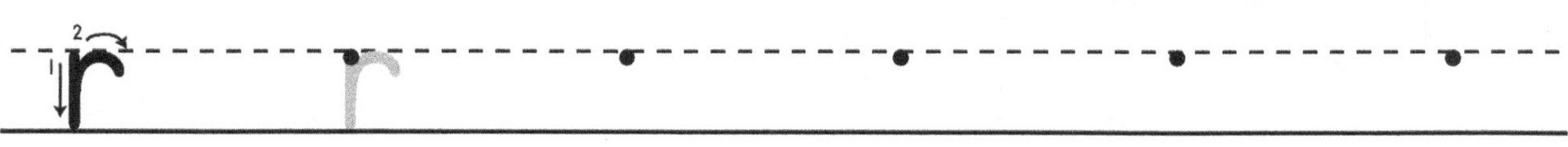

If your family has pets, make a chart to show things that your child can do to help take care of them. Put a star sticker on the chart each time your child completes one of the items. If your family doesn't have pets, visit a family that does. Ask if your child can help feed the other family's pet during the visit.

Take It Away

Draw a picture to solve each problem.
For example:

$8 - 4 =$ 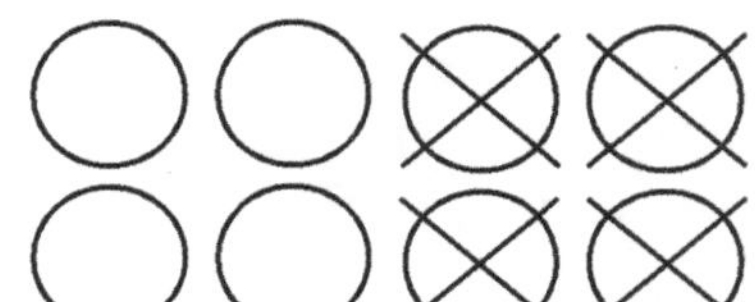

1.	$7-2=$
2.	$8-5=$
3.	$9-3=$
4.	$10-4=$
5.	$6-2=$
6.	$10-5=$

Remove the face cards from a deck of cards. Shuffle the numbered cards and place them face down in a stack. Take turns with your child picking one card from the top of the stack. The person with the larger number subtracts the smaller number. Continue playing until all the cards are used.

Tell Me About It

An adjective is a word that describes something. Trace the word. Draw pictures of things that match each adjective.

1. tall	2. red
3. soft	4. hot

Trace and write.

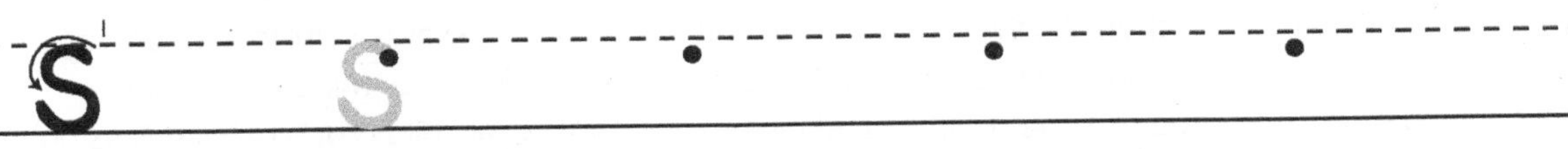

Have your child select a toy. Together make a list of adjectives that describe the toy.

The Big Ten

Fill in the number chart from 1 to 30.

1						7			
		13							20
				25				29	

Subtract. Use the chart for help.

1.	17 − 10 =	26 − 10 =
2.	21 − 10 =	11 − 10 =
3.	14 − 10 =	13 − 10 =
4.	28 − 10 =	24 − 10 =
5.	15 − 10 =	18 − 10 =
6.	23 − 10 =	20 − 10 =

Explain to your child that a number chart like the one shown on this page can be a very useful tool for adding and subtracting 10. Point to any number on the chart. Say the name of the number and "minus ten." Then demonstrate how to move your finger up one space to find the answer. Have your child practice this skill using a different number each time. Then switch to addition and show how you move your finger down one space to add 10.

How to Plant a Flower

Listen to the poem about growing flowers. Draw a picture for each step.

1. Dig a hole.	2. Drop in seeds.
3. Cover with dirt.	4. Wait and see.
5. Sprinkle water.	6. Soak up sun.
7. Here come flowers.	8. Oh what fun!

Trace and write.

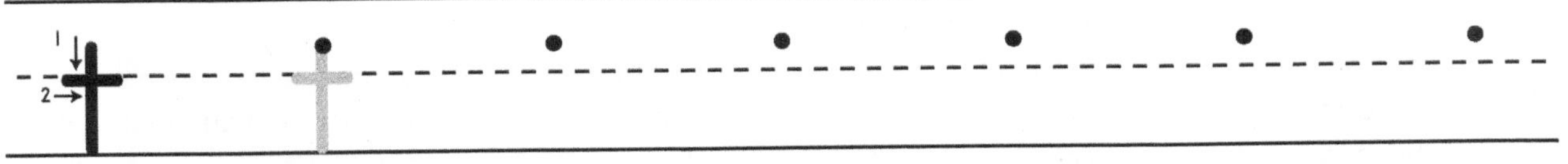

Have your child identify the different steps involved in an activity, such as getting dressed, making a sandwich, or getting ready for bed. Write a sentence and draw a simple picture for each step. Then cut the sentences apart, mix them up, and challenge your child to put them back in order again.

All in the Family

Solve.

1. 2, 4, 6	2+4= 4+2=	6−2= 6−4=
2. 1, 2, 3	1+2= 2+1=	3−1= 3−2=
3. 3, 5, 8	3+5= 5+3=	8−3= 8−5=
4. 4, 1, 5	1+4= 4+1=	5−1= 5−4=

Cut squares and triangles out of construction paper. Tell your child that the shapes will be used to make a house for different "fact families." Explain that each fact family can only have three numbers in it and that all the numbers have to work together to make true math sentences. To make the house, glue one triangle roof to the top of one square house. Write the numbers 1, 2, and 3 on the triangle. Then have your child tell you the math sentences that can be made using those three numbers (1 + 2 = 3, 2 + 1 = 3, 3 – 1 = 2, and 3 – 2 = 1). Record the sentences on the square part of the house. Challenge your child to think of more fact families and make a different house for each one.

Hickory, Dickory, Dock

Listen to the nursery rhyme.

Hickory, dickory, dock,
The mouse ran up the clock.
The clock struck one,
The mouse ran down,
Hickory, dickory, dock.

- Traditional

Talk about it.

1. Who ran up the clock?
2. What time was it when the mouse ran down?
3. Draw a picture of something you do at around 1:00 each day.
4. *Mouse* starts with *m*. Say as many words as you can that also start with *m*.

Trace and write.

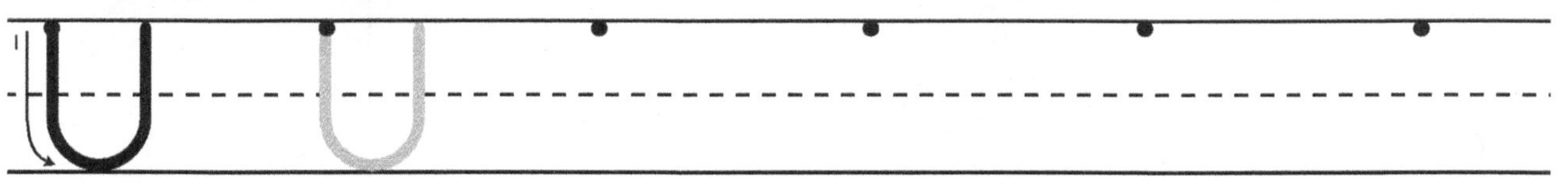

Use the Internet to find and print a set of clock faces. Cut the clocks out and glue each one to a separate sheet of paper. Draw clock hands on the clocks to show different times. Staple the pages together and have your child illustrate each page to show something he or she does at the time shown on the clock.

Shape Up

Color each picture that has the same shape.

1.

2.

3.

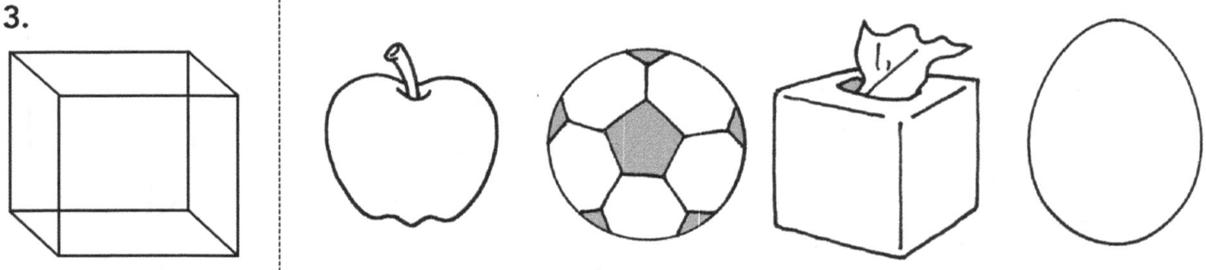

4.

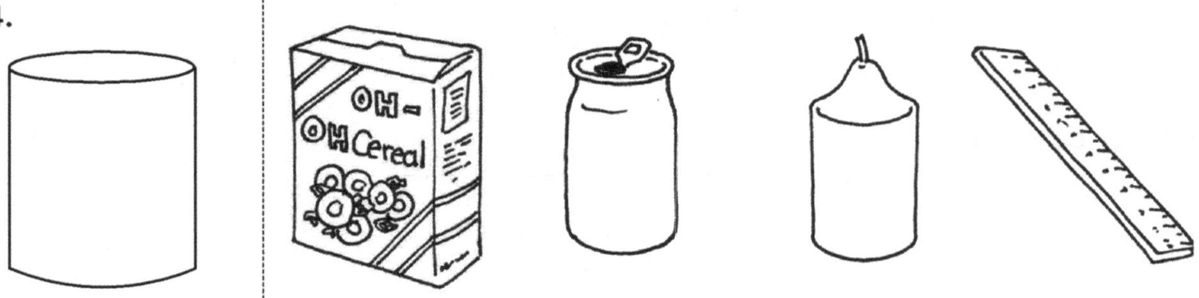

Have your child look through the house for things that are the shape of a cone, sphere, cube, or cylinder. Have him or her sort the objects by shape.

A Star in the Family

Interview someone in your family. Color the star when you have asked the person a question that begins with the word shown.

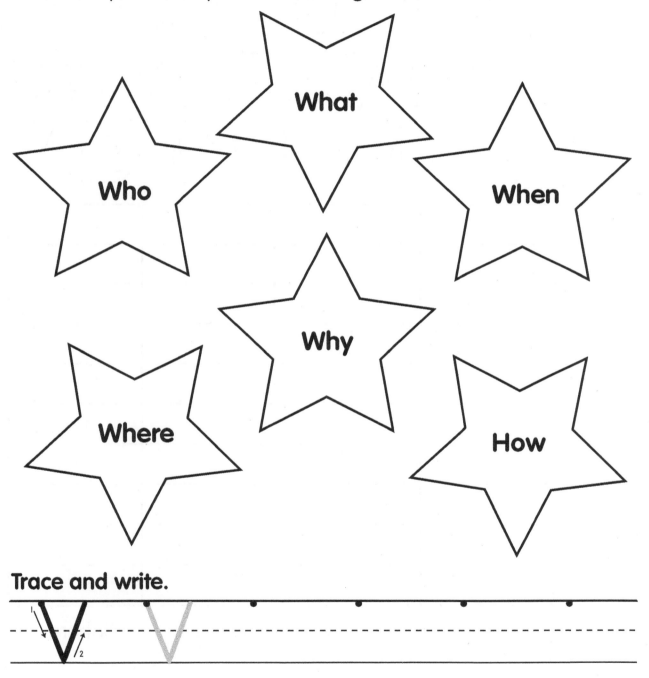

What

Who

When

Why

Where

How

Trace and write.

V V

Write each question word on a separate sticker. Attach the stickers to different sections of a game spinner. Then read a story to your child and have your child spin the spinner after each page or two. Ask your child a question about the story that begins with the question word the spinner stopped on.

Make a Graph

Count the shapes. Color a box for each shape.

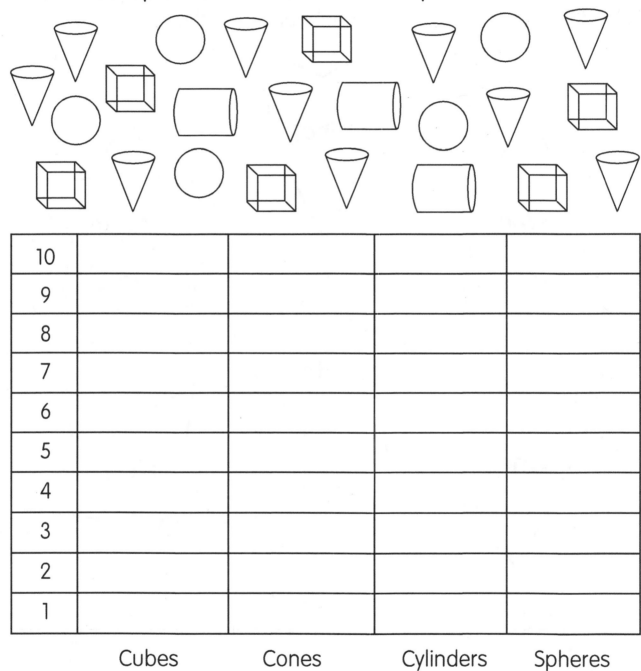

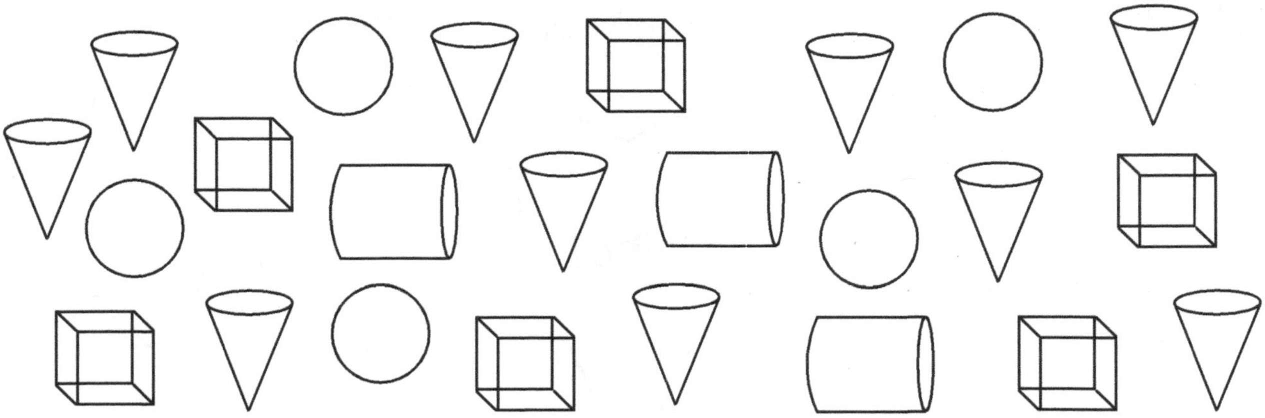

10				
9				
8				
7				
6				
5				
4				
3				
2				
1				
	Cubes	Cones	Cylinders	Spheres

Help your child hunt through your pantry to find foods that represent different shapes. For example, use tortilla chips for triangles, marshmallows for cylinders, and cheese balls for spheres. Have your child categorize the foods by shape and count how many are in each category.

Firefighters

Listen to the story.

Firefighters help their communities. They teach people about fire safety. They make sure buildings have smoke detectors and fire sprinklers. They help people who are sick or hurt. They put out fires. Firefighters are heroes.

Talk about it.

1. What are ways that firefighters help the community?
2. Why are firefighters heroes?
3. Name another worker that helps the community.

Trace and write.

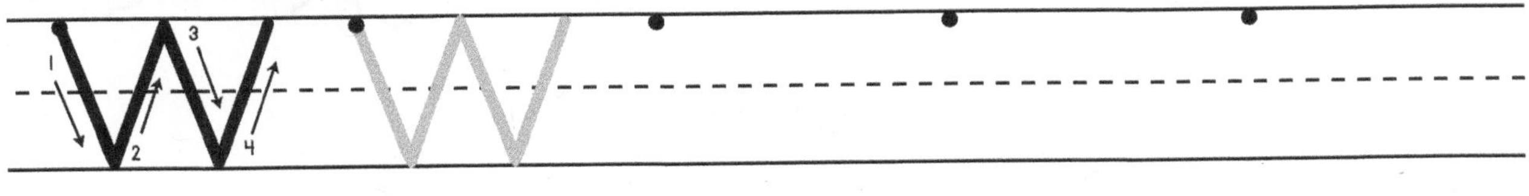

Call your local fire department and ask about taking a tour of the fire station. With a small group, you and your child can learn more about fire safety and the work that firefighters do.

Cute Caterpillars

Use pennies to measure the length of each caterpillar.

1. 

_______________ pennies long

2. 

_______________ pennies long

3. 

_______________ pennies long

4. 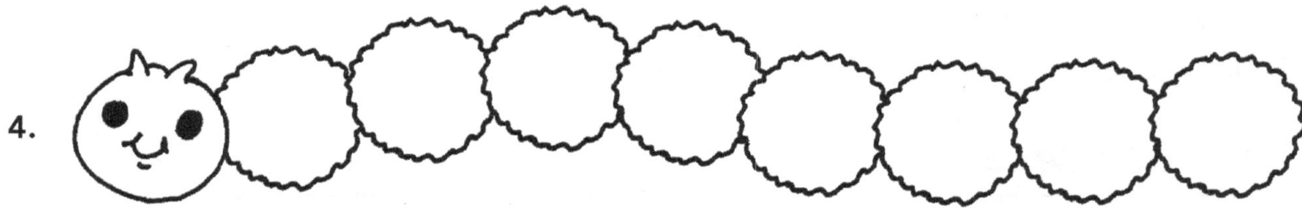

_______________ pennies long

Let your child use pennies, cereal pieces, paper clips, and other non-standard objects to measure different things in your house. Have your child compare the results from using different measuring tools to measure the same object. For example, the same book might measure 10 pennies long or 15 paper clips long.

What's at School?

Circle the things you would find at school. Cross out the things you would not find at school. Color the pictures.

Trace and write.

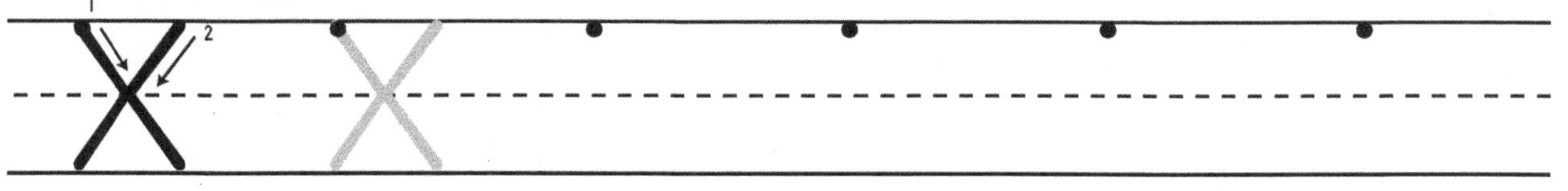

Name a place your child is familiar with, such as a park or restaurant. Then name things that can be found in that place. Instruct your child to make a buzzer sound when you name things that don't belong.

Woof, Woof!

Write how many inches long each dog is.

1.

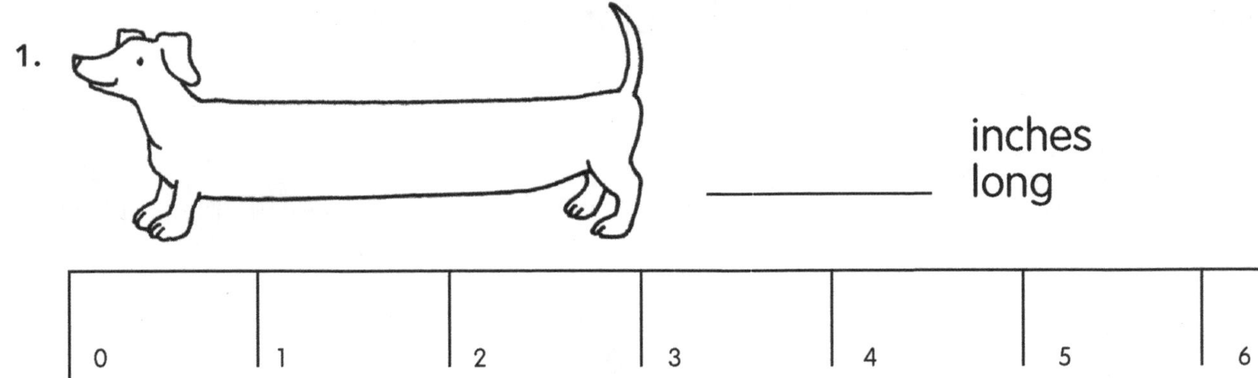

_________ inches long

2.

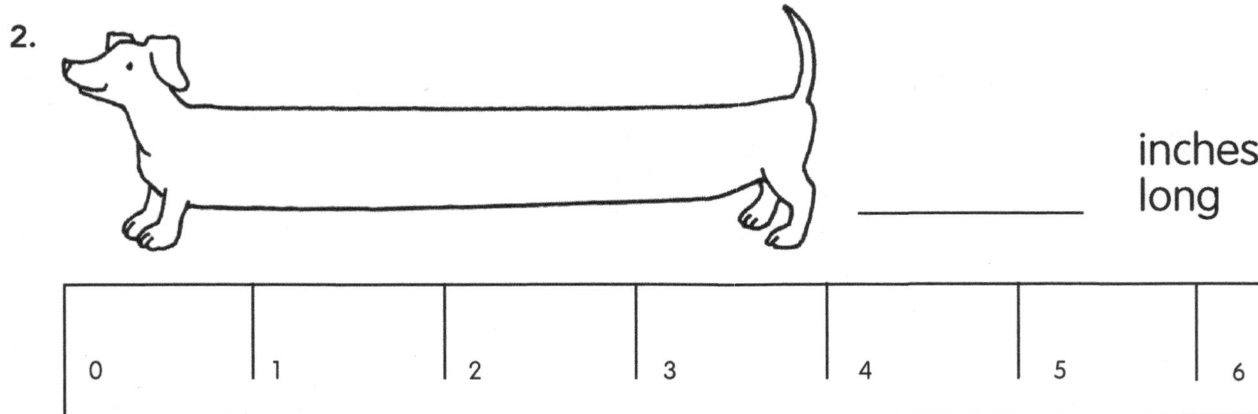

_________ inches long

3.

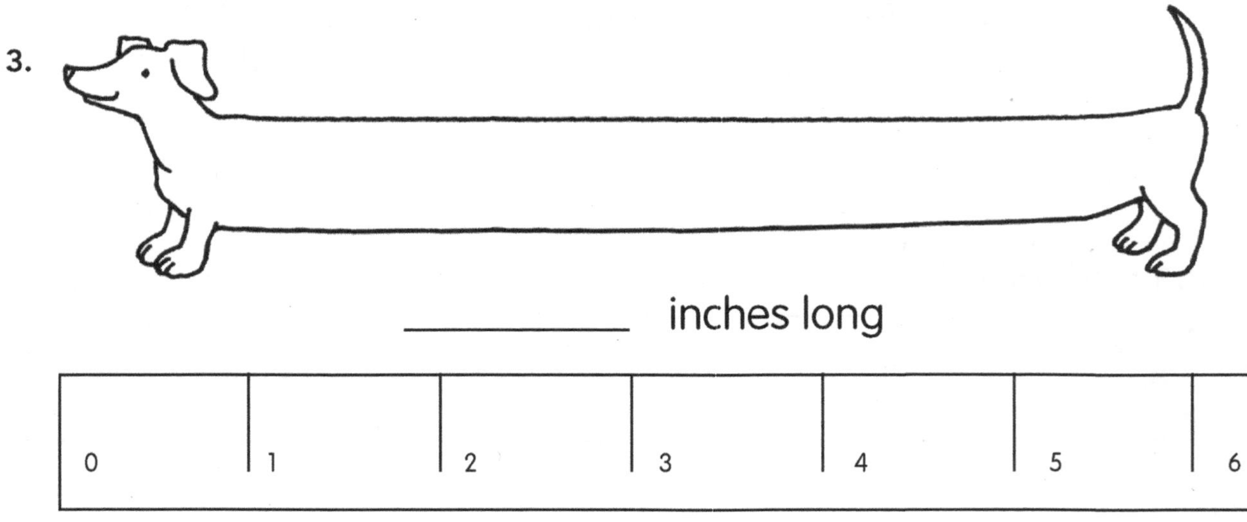

_________ inches long

Let your child use a flexible tape measure to practice standard measurement of a variety of objects.

Time to Wash

Listen to the poem.

Swish-swash! It's time to wash!
What should we wash today?
Fingers and toes,
A neck and a nose,
Each pair of arms and legs.
Two ears and a chin,
All of your skin.
Now let's go run and play!

Talk about it.

1. What is this poem about?
2. What are other things that people wash besides themselves?
3. What happens at the end of the poem?

Trace and write.

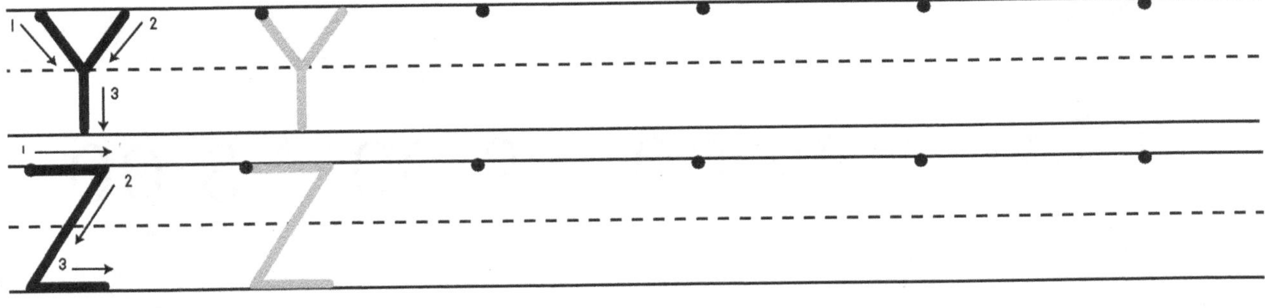

Have your child underline each word in the poem that is a part of the body. Then have him or her name other body parts as you write the words. Point out the beginning and ending sound of each word.

Tick Tock

Circle the time shown on each clock.

1. 	12:00	3:00	5:00
2. 	6:00	9:00	2:00
3. 	1:00	4:00	2:00
4. 	4:00	7:00	10:00
5. 	8:00	11:00	7:00
6. 	12:00	9:00	3:00

Help your child make a clock from a paper plate. Write the numbers from 1 to 12 around the edges of the plate. Cut clock hands from construction paper and attach them to the center of the plate with a brass paper fastener.

How Many Days Has My Baby To Play?

Listen to the nursery rhyme.

How many days has my baby to play?
Saturday, Sunday, Monday,
Tuesday, Wednesday, Thursday, Friday,
Saturday, Sunday, Monday.

- Traditional

Talk about it.

1. How many days are named in this rhyme? Count them.
2. Why do you think Saturday, Sunday, and Monday are named twice?
3. What is your favorite day of the week? What do you like to do on that day?
4. The days of the week start with capital letters. Circle all of the capital letters in the rhyme.

Trace and write.

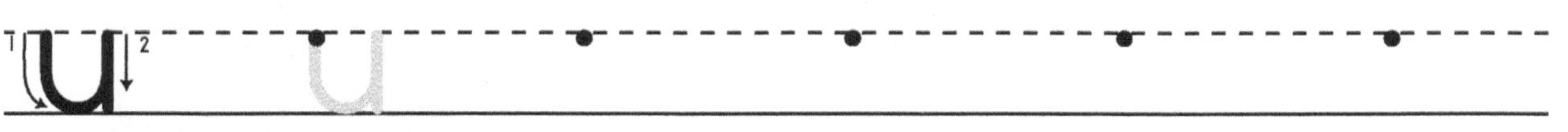

Print a blank month-long calendar from the Internet. Help your child write in the numbers for each day of the month. Mark the date for the first day of school and have your child count how many days away it is until then.

All in a Day's Work

Write the name of the day that is missing from each list. Use the words in the box to help.

Sunday Monday Tuesday Wednesday Thursday Friday Saturday

1.	Tuesday, ______________________ , Thursday
2.	Sunday, Monday, ______________________
3.	Wednesday, Thursday, ______________________
4.	______________________ , Monday, Tuesday
5.	Friday, ______________________ , Sunday
6.	Sunday, ______________________ , Tuesday
7.	______________________ , Friday, Saturday

Show your child a calendar and point to today's date. Say, "Today is (name the day of the week)." Ask, "What was yesterday? What will tomorrow be?" Each day, have your child practice identifying the days of the week for today, yesterday, and tomorrow.

Here I Go!

Write the words.

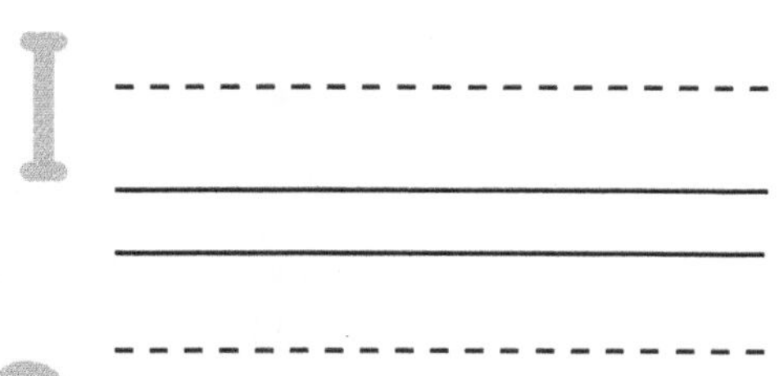

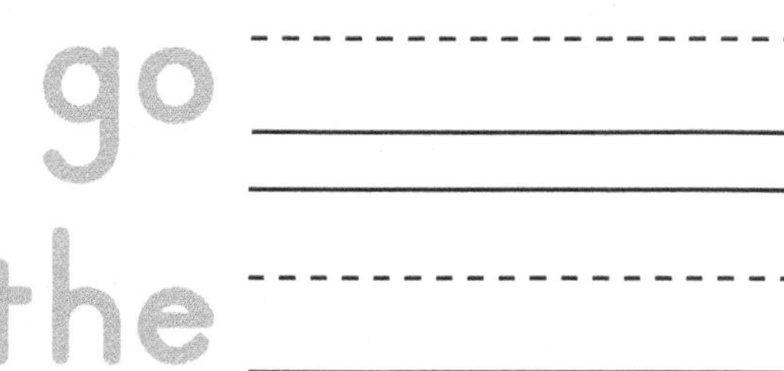

Read the sentences.

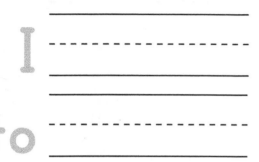

1. I go to the  park .

2. I go to the  school .

3. I go to the  house .

4. I go to the  store .

Trace and write.

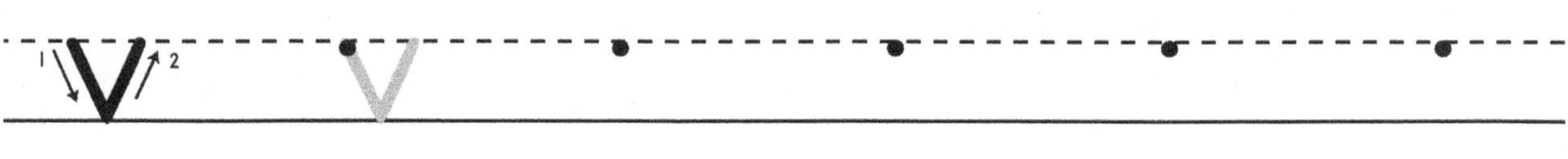

Make a memory match game using the four sight words on this page. Write each word on two separate cards. Shuffle the cards and arrange them face-down on a table. Have your child flip two cards over on each turn to find the matching words. Be sure to encourage your child to read the words on the cards.

Hot Summer Days

Use the calendar to answer the questions.

August

SUNDAY	MONDAY	TUESDAY	WEDNESDAY	THURSDAY	FRIDAY	SATURDAY
	1	2	3	4	5	6
7	8	9	10	11	12	13
14	15	16	17	18	19	20
21	22	23	24	25	26	27
28	29	30	31			

1. What month is it? ______________________

2. How many Mondays are there in the month? ______________________

3. Are there more Tuesdays or Saturdays? ______________________

4. On what day of the week is August 1? ______________________

5. What date is the last day of this month?
____

Let your child look through a 12-month calendar. Have him or her mark special days throughout the year, like family birthdays, holidays, vacations, the first day of school, and so on.

Frogs and Toads

Listen to the story.

Frogs and toads are a lot alike. They live on land and in water. They have sticky tongues for catching food. They make croaking sounds.

Frogs and toads are different too. Frogs have smooth, wet skin. Toads have bumpy, dry skin. Frogs have long, skinny back legs. This helps them jump far. Toads have short, thick back legs. They take short hops.

Talk about it.

1. How are frogs and toads alike?
2. How are frogs and toads different?

Label the pictures—frog or toad.

Trace and write.

Encourage your child to compare and contrast two other animals that are similar, such as crocodiles and alligators or monkeys and apes. Together read library books about the animals and list the ways each pair is alike and different.

Funny Bunnies

How many bunny ears? Count by twos.

1. 2	2.
3.	4.
5.	6.

Help your child learn to count by fives. Point out that there are five fingers on one hand. Paint your child's hand and have him or her make handprints across a sheet of paper. Point to the handprints, counting by fives as you go *(5, 10, 15, 20,* and so on).

Read, Write, Find

Trace and write the words.

and ______ was ______

said ______ you ______

Find the words in the puzzle. They go across and down.

a	j	k	c	h	e	m
n	f	w	a	s	n	y
d	p	b	q	t	g	o
l	s	a	i	d	r	u

Trace and write.

X x

y y

Z z

Write the word *and* on a card. Ask your child what word it would become if you wrote a *b* in front of it (*band*). Substitute the letter *b* for another consonant like *s* (*sand*). Continue with more letters, then different single-syllable words like *at, bed,* and *it.*

Sweet Strawberries

Circle sets of 10. Write how many tens and ones. Write the number.

1.

tens	ones

2.

tens	ones

3.

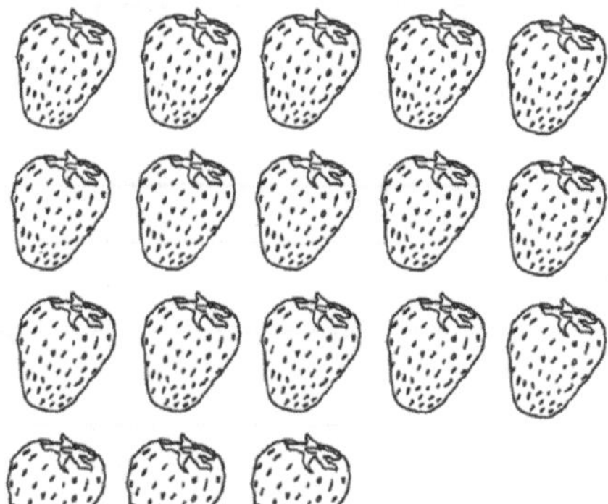

tens	ones

Give your child 10 craft sticks. Have him or her glue 10 beans on each stick. Help your child use the sticks to count by 10 to 100. Then call out numbers that are less than 30 and have your child use the sticks and loose beans to show that number. For example, the number 23 would be shown with two sticks (20) and three loose beans (3).

Listen to the poem.
Draw clothes on the teddy bear to show one of the outfits listed.

Teddy Bear, Teddy Bear

Teddy Bear, Teddy Bear,
What should you wear?

The blue sailor suit
And red cowboy boots?
The green soccer shirt
And pink, sparkly skirt?
The brown overalls
And orange and white shawl?

Teddy Bear, Teddy Bear,
Here's what to wear!
A polka-dot bow in your hair.

Write your first and last name.

The first day of Kindergarten is almost here! Help your child put together different outfits to choose from for the big day. Talk about the colors, patterns, and styles that work well together. Let your child have fun trying on and modeling the different selections.

Race to 100

Have each player choose a marker. Players take turns rolling two dice, adding the numbers together, and moving the marker that many spaces on the board. The first player to get to 100 wins!

1	2	3	4	5	6	7	8	9	10
11	12	13	14	15	16	17	18	19	20
21	22	23	24	25	26	27	28	29	30
31	32	33	34	35	36	37	38	39	40
41	42	43	44	45	46	47	48	49	50
51	52	53	54	55	56	57	58	59	60
61	62	63	64	65	66	67	68	69	70
71	72	73	74	75	76	77	78	79	80
81	82	83	84	85	86	87	88	89	90
91	92	93	94	95	96	97	98	99	100

A Hundreds Chart can be used for lots of number awareness games. Try this one: Choose a number (*33*). Give clues to see if your child can guess the number *(The number is greater than 32 and less than 34; It is below 23 on the chart and above 43; If you add 3 to 30, you will find it,* and so on.) Let your child have a turn giving you clues about a number as well.

Answer Key

Page 9
1. The black sheep
2. Answers will vary.
3. Master is the sheep's male owner and dame is the sheep's female owner.
4. Circled words should include: Baa, baa, black, bags, boy, Baa, baa, black, bags.

Page 10

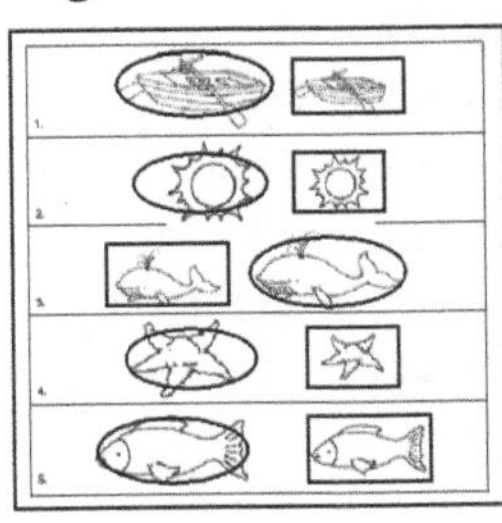

Page 11

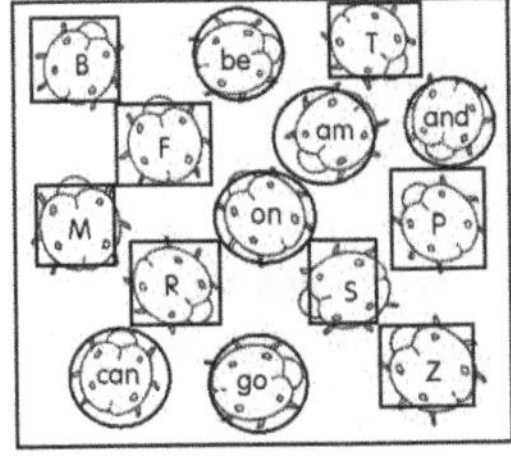

Page 12

Page 13
1. In the woods
2. Frogs live in the pond. Answers will vary for other pond animals.
3. Answers will vary.

Page 14

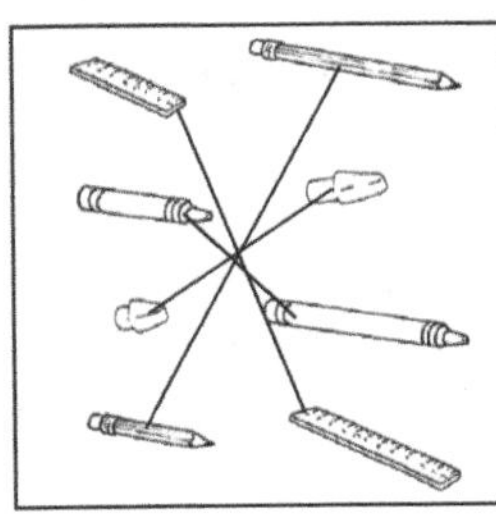

Page 15
Child should color the shells if the letters can be named. They should circle the shells if the letters cannot be named.

Page 16
The following pictures should be colored:
1. horse
2. man
3. tree
4. penny
5. butterfly
6. spider

Page 17
1. The alphabet
2. Child should circle the letters that he or she can name.

Page 18

Page 19
1. On a wall
2. Answers will vary.
3. Answers will vary.
4. Circled words should include: sat, a, wall, had, a, great, fall, All, And, all, again.

Page 21

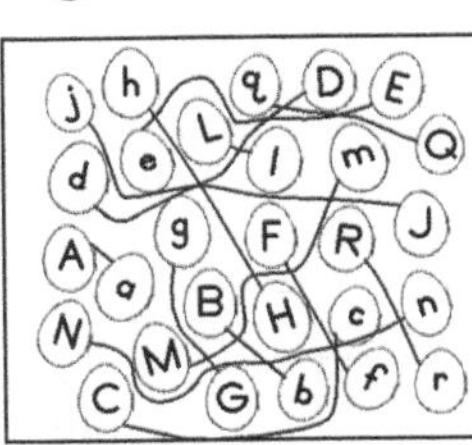

Page 23
1. After breakfast and before bedtime
2. Put toothpaste on the toothbrush
3. No, you should brush every side of every tooth
4. Answers will vary.

Page 25

Page 27
1. On a farm
2. The dogs
3. Pictures should be colored.
4. Words should be circled.

Page 28

Page 29
1. Because it twinkles
2. When the sun is gone
3. Answers will vary.
4. Circled words should include: star, are, high, sky, gone, upon, light, night.

Page 30
The following pictures complete the patterns:
1. star
2. moon
3. sun
4. rainbow
5. cloud

Page 31
The following pictures should be colored:
1. hat, bat
2. men, ten
3. jar, car
4. rug, mug
5. ring, swing

Page 32
The following shapes complete the patterns:
1. diamond
2. circle
3. rectangle
4. square
5. triangle

Page 33
1. Hats
2. A hard hat that keeps the head safe.

Page 34
Child should color the pictures to make a pattern. Patterns will vary.

Page 35
Lines should be drawn between the following:
duck, truck
cake, rake
mouse, house
fox, box
tree, bee

Page 36

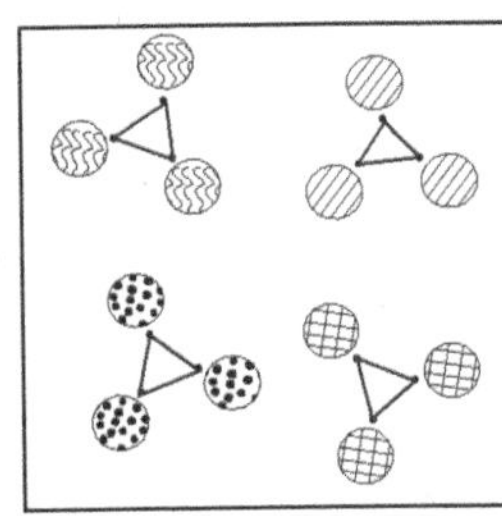

Page 37
Child should mark the words in the poem as follows:

Here is the

1. Toys
2. doll, ball; truck, duck; bear, share
3. They are supposed to share them.

Page 38
Quilt should be colored. Patterns used will vary.

Page 39
1. Little Jack Horner
2. Answers will vary.
3. A plum; answers will vary.
4. Circled words should include: pie, put, plum.

Page 40

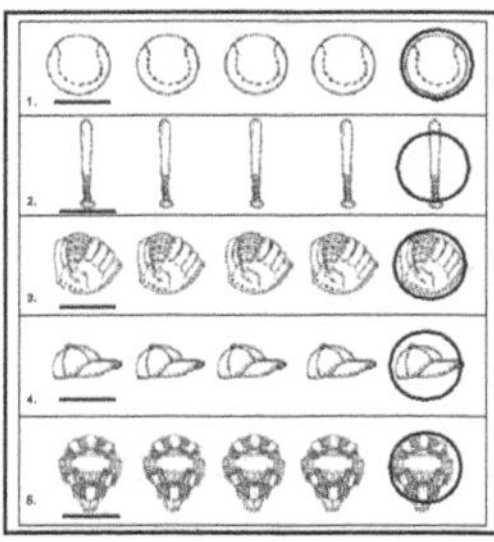

Page 41
1. t
2. s
3. r
4. d
5. c
6. b

Page 42
The number of scoops drawn on each cone should match the number printed on the cone.

Page 43
1. The pony ride
2. The merry-go-round
3. Four tickets
4. Answers will vary.

Page 44
1. 7
2. 8
3. 10
4. 6
5. 9

Page 45
The following pictures should be colored:
1. fish, feather
2. pig, pumpkin
3. gate, girl
4. mop, monkey
5. horse, house
6. lamb, leaf

Page 46

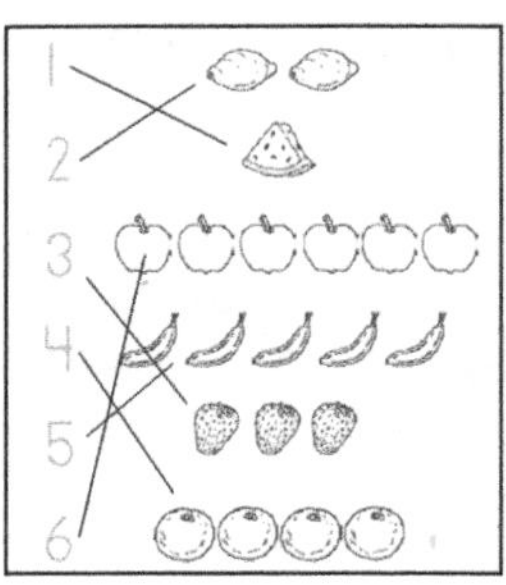

Page 47
Child should mark the words in the poem as follows:

the

1. fruit salad
2. apples, cherries
3. Answers will vary.

Page 48

Page 49
1. John's mother or father
2. pants
3. Answers will vary.
4. Circled words should include: Diddle, diddle, dumpling, Diddle, diddle, dumpling.

Page 50

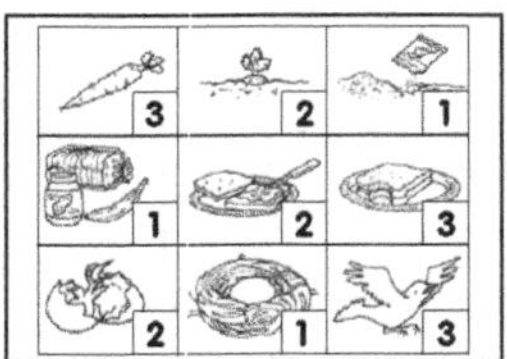

Page 51

Page 52
Answers will vary based on child's individual experiences.

Page 53
1. Puppies are different because of their sizes, types of hair, and types of ears.
2. Puppies are alike because they like to play, make friends, take naps, and explore.
3. Answers will vary.

Page 54
The following pictures should be crossed out:
1. doll
2. pencil
3. quarter
4. rabbit

Page 55
Answers will vary.

Page 56
Child should use position words to describe where things in the picture are located.

Page 57
Kites should be colored to match the color words in the poem. Child should draw a picture in the box that shows kites.

Page 58
Pictures will vary.

Page 59
1. A shoe is buckled.
2. sticks
3. Answers will vary.
4. Circled words should include: two, shoe; four, door; six, sticks; eight, straight; ten, hen.

Page 60

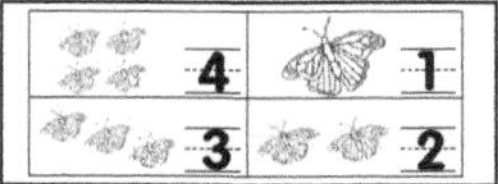

Page 61

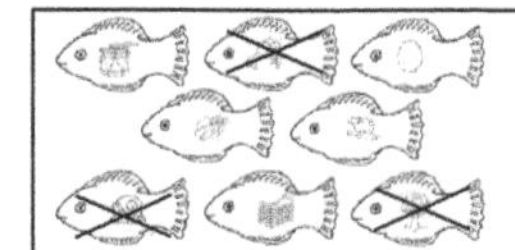

Page 62

6	7
5	8

Page 63
1. eyes, ears, nose, mouth, and skin
2. eyes and ears
3. nose, mouth, skin

Page 64

9	12
11	10

Page 65

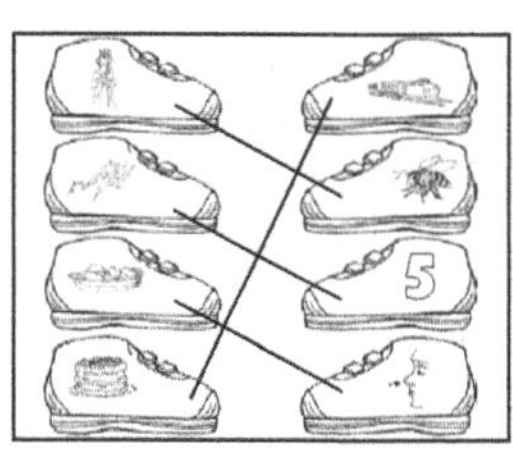

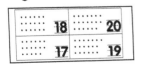

Page 66

14	15
16	13

Page 67
1. There is a surprise party for Hen.
2. Answers will vary but may include farm animals.
3. So they can surprise Hen.
4. Hen's
5. Number words should be circled in the poem.

Page 68

18	20
17	19

Page 69
1. To take care of the sheep
2. because Little Boy Blue fell asleep
3. under the haystack
4. Circled words should include: Boy, Blue, come, blow, cow's, corn, boy.

Page 70
1. 1 + 2 = 3
2. 1 + 3 = 4
3. 3 + 1 = 4
4. 1 + 1 = 2
5. 1 + 0 = 1

Page 71
These pictures should be circled: farmer, girl. These pictures should be underlined: park, school. These pictures should have a box around them: pumpkin, plane. Pictures of nouns drawn will vary.

Page 72
1. 4+1=5
2. 2+1=3
3. 1+1=2
4. 3+1=4
5. 6+1=7
6. 5+1=6

Page 73
Paths drawn will vary.

Page 74
1. 4 + 4 = 8
2. 2 + 2 = 4
3. 5 + 5 = 10
4. 3 + 3 = 6
5. 1 + 1 = 2
6. 6 + 6 = 12

Page 76
Possible answers include:
7: 0 + 7, 1 + 6, 2 + 5, 3 + 4, 4 + 3, 5 + 2, 6 + 1, 7 + 0.

8: 0 + 8, 1 + 7, 2 + 6, 3 + 5, 4 + 4, 5 + 3, 6 + 2, 7 + 1, 8 + 0.

9: 0 + 9, 1 + 8, 2 + 7, 3 + 6, 4 + 5, 5 + 4, 6 + 3, 7 + 2, 8 + 1, 9 + 0.

10: 0 + 10, 1 + 9, 2 + 8, 3 + 7, 4 + 6, 5 + 5, 6 + 4, 7 + 3, 8 + 2, 9 + 1, 10 + 0

Page 77
1. in a tree
2. in a row, high and low
3. waving
4. Circled words should include: row, low; tree, me.

Page 78
1. 6 + 4 = 10
2. 3 + 7 = 10
3. 5 + 5 = 10
4. 7 + 3 = 10
5. 4 + 6 = 10

Page 79
1. in a house
2. stop
3. Answers will vary.
4. Answers will vary.

Page 80
1. 5 – 2 = 3
2. 4 – 3 = 1
3. 2 – 2 = 0
4. 5 – 3 = 2
5. 3 – 1= 2
6. 4 – 1 = 3

Page 81
1. swim
2. run
3. sleep
4. sing
5. read
6. jump

Page 82
1. 2
2. 4
3. 5
4. 1
5. 3
6. 0

Page 83
1. pets
2. They need to be played with, brushed, and given exercise, food, and water.
3. a cat
4. Answers will vary.

Page 84
Pictures will vary.
1. 5
2. 3
3. 6
4. 6
5. 4
6. 5

Page 85
Pictures will vary.

Page 86

1	2	3	4	5	6	7	8	9	10
11	12	13	14	15	16	17	18	19	20
21	22	23	24	25	26	27	28	29	30

1. 7, 16
2. 11, 1
3. 4, 3
4. 18, 14
5. 5, 8
6. 13, 10

Page 87
Pictures will vary.

Page 88
1. 2 + 4 = 6
   4 + 2 = 6
   6 – 2 = 4
   6 – 4 = 2

2. 1 + 2 = 3
   2 + 1 = 3
   3 – 1 = 2
   3 – 2 = 1

3. 3 + 5 = 8
   5 + 3 = 8
   8 – 3 = 5
   8 – 5 = 3

4. 1 + 4 = 5
   4 + 1 = 5
   5 – 1 = 4
   5 – 4 = 1

Page 89
1. a mouse
2. 1:00
3. Pictures will vary.
4. Words will vary.

Page 90
The following pictures should be colored:
1. party hat, megaphone
2. orange, globe
3. tissue box
4. can, candle

Page 91
Questions will vary.

Page 92

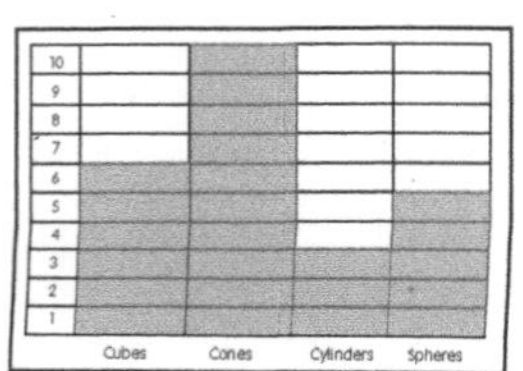

Page 93
1. Any of the following: They teach about fire safety. They make sure buildings have smoke detectors and fire sprinklers. They help people who are hurt or sick. They put out fires.
2. Answers will vary.
3. Answers will vary.

Page 94
1. 6
2. 7
3. 8
4. 9

Page 95

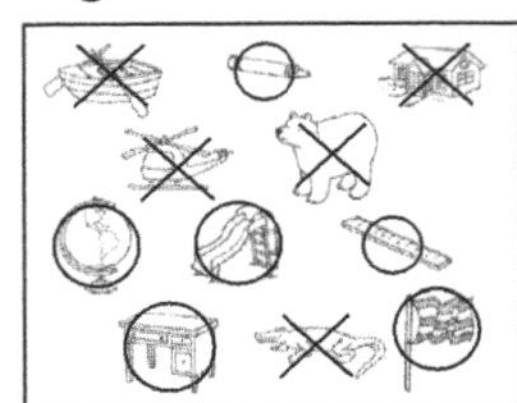

Page 96
1. 3 inches long
2. 4 inches long
3. 6 inches long

Page 97
1. Taking a bath
2. Answers will vary.
3. They finish the bath and go play.

Page 98
1. 3:00
2. 6:00
3. 2:00
4. 4:00
5. 7:00
6. 9:00

Page 99
1. 10
2. Answers will vary.
3. Answers will vary.
4. The word How and each day of the week should have its first letter circled.

Page 100
1. Wednesday
2. Tuesday
3. Friday
4. Sunday
5. Saturday
6. Monday
7. Thursday

Page 102
1. August
2. 5
3. Tuesdays
4. Monday
5. Wednesday, August 31

Page 103
1. Any of the following: They live on land and in water. They have sticky tongues for catching food. They make croaking sounds.
2. Any of the following: Frogs have smooth, wet skin, long, skinny back legs, and they can jump far. Toads have bumpy, dry skin, short, thick back legs, and take short hops.

Page 104
1. 2
2. 4
3. 6
4. 8
5. 10
6. 12

Page 105

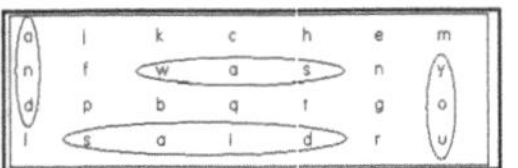

Page 106

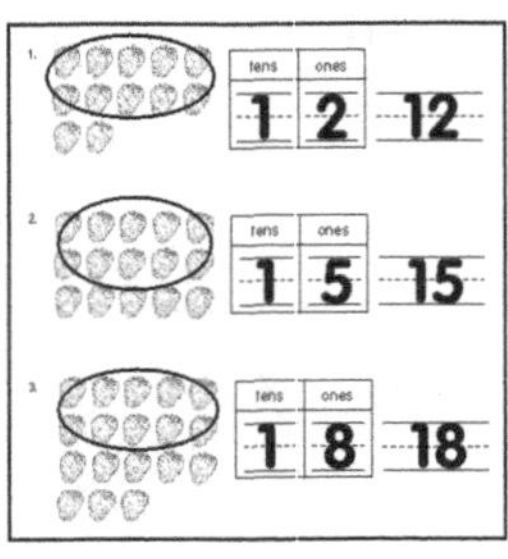

Page 107
Child should draw clothes on the teddy bear.